SHA

welcome

SHA, ITS STORY AND ITS REASON FOR BEING

To a great extent, our development and health, from the moment we are conceived, depends on the food we eat. More often than not, however, contemporary society ignores the vital importance of this fact. Education varies depending on each country's state of development, but in general our educational systems provide us with an endless amount of knowledge so that we may acquire a minimum level of culture that will be useful to us in life. Except for certain notable exceptions, however, we are taught little or nothing about healthy nutrition so that we are able to take care of our own health, something that would bring great benefits to all of society and even to the public coffers.

The planet's huge economic inequalities and the lack of dependable information means that while a significant part of the world's population is dying of hunger, another part suffers from a range of serious illnesses caused by overeating. More than 800 million people in the world suffer from chronic hunger and it is, among other miseries, the primary cause of death for children under the age of five around the world. More than 2 billion people suffer from lack of micronutrients while at the same time more than 600 million people are either overweight or obese, leading to numerous illnesses and deaths. Additionally, the latter, despite being overfed, often suffer from important nutritional deficiencies, and both of these extremes can cause a variety of health problems.

In light of this, it's completely normal for almost all of us to have health problems at some point in our lives and, sadly, due to the lack of accurate information, we often don't understand that these problems are often related to our habits and, fundamentally, to what we eat. Unfortunately, the majority of physicians

> The World Health Organization and most governmental health agencies agree that between 60% and 75% of all deaths are caused by poor nutrition, lack of exercise and lack of exercise and smoking.

are likewise ignorant of this relationship and both they and their loved ones suffer from the same health problems as the rest of the population, resorting to medication or surgery to cure them.

For many years of my life, I was a typical example of this system. Over a period of almost thirty years I suffered from different health problems that conditioned my quality of life. I visited endless specialists who, after many examinations, diagnosed different pathologies that didn't always coincide with one another, and these specialists prescribed medication that didn't cure my symptoms and discomfort. Thus, my problem grew, the symptoms got worse, and I even received a very worrying diagnosis. Luckily, however, a friend told me about a highly knowledgeable doctor of nutrition and natural medicine. I visited him and thanks to his nutritional advice, within a few weeks I was able to reach a state of health that I'd believed was hopelessly out of reach. I permanently rid myself of those symptoms that I'd assumed were chronic and I recovered a vitality and energy I'd only known in my youth. After this experience, I began to investigate the most effective and proven natural therapies and the enormous importance of nutrition in human beings. I discovered, with scientific information from some of the world's best universities, how mistaken I was about my food beliefs; the more I researched, the more surprised I became. I found it hard to believe that so much ignorance existed in society, even among many health professionals.

I was sorry that I hadn't discovered this knowledge many years earlier, not so much because I'd suffered unnecessarily for three decades, but rather because I'd seen loved ones, such as my mother, my aunt, my sister, my father-in-law and some of my friends, a little over the age of fifty, suffer and die from cancer and other illnesses that, to a large extent, were related to a poor diet. From that moment on, a need and a commitment awoke in me to share and popularize this excellent and proven knowledge about nutrition and natural therapies, although without disregarding in the least the great achievements of

conventional medicine, where it respects the holistic quality of human health, and always giving priority to natural therapies that, wisely applied, strengthen the fantastic self-curing capacity of the human body.

With the support of my family, we began to work toward this dream, today a reality, searching for excellence in every aspect, every detail, seeking out recognized, international experts in all of the areas that may be susceptible to poor nutrition.

The importance of this subject is such that if one day we are able to spread and massively apply this knowledge, the transformation of the world would be so great it would be unrecognizable to us, and I don't believe I'm exaggerating. Poor nutrition – call it malnutrition, a lack of micronutrients, being overweight, obesity and chemical agents – not only affects people's health and wellbeing, but it also has a huge effect on one's physical and cognitive development, weakening the immunological system, increasing one's susceptibility to contagious and non-contagious diseases, limiting one's true human potential in addition to having tremendous social, economic and environmental impacts.

Governments find themselves forced to increase spending on health, more hospitals are built every year, more money is spent on medicine and there are more and more cases of cancer and other diseases. World Health Organization forecasts are alarming: within a few years, one in three people will get cancer, when just 90 years ago in the United States only one in thirty people was diagnosed with cancer. Today, in Spain, it is predicated that one of out of every two children born today will get cancer.

Unfortunately, the socio-economic changes involved in applying the knowledge that we use daily at SHA would be so revolutionary that it's very unlikely a government would dare to try it, even if it were convinced of the enormous health benefits it would bring.

Representatives of the Food and Agriculture Organization of the United Nations (FAO) and the World Health Organization (WHO) met in Rome on November 19-21, 2014, at the Second International Conference on Nutrition (ICN2) which was jointly organized by these two organizations. There they addressed the many challenges posed by malnutrition in all its forms and established ways to face them in the coming decades. They also recognized, among other things, that certain socioeconomic and environmental changes can have an effect on eating habits and physical activity, leading to a greater susceptibility to obesity and non-contagious diseases due to increasingly sedentary lifestyles and a greater intake of foods high in saturated fats and trans fats, sugar, salt and sodium.

This is not news. However, legislation in nearly all of the member states allows hundreds of thousands of tons of these foods that end up making their consumers, even the most vulnerable, such as children, pregnant women and the elderly, sick to be marketed and sold.

FAO also recognizes that current food systems face increasing difficulty in providing sufficient food that is safe, diverse and rich in nutrients that together contribute to a healthy diet. This difficulty is due, among other things, to limitations arising from a scarcity of resources, environmental deterioration and unsustainable production models. Fundamentally, the problem is caused by increased meat consumption, which results in a generalized degradation of health and serious environmental problems. According to the United States Department of Agriculture, half of the fish caught worldwide is used in animal feed.

SHA isn't just another brand dedicated to health or tourism. Since its foundation, its concerns have gone far beyond this and include such important matters as how to contribute to the future sustainability of the planet, proposing changes that make a significant increase in the healthy food resources needed so badly by millions of undernourished people and those who die of hunger possible.

To get an idea of the magnitude of the problem, I will refer to certain figures that, while apparently boring, clearly illustrate our current predicament.

Animal production consumes 25 times more energy and natural resources than the resources needed to produce the same amount of vegetable protein.

For every 16 kilos of grains and vegetables given to cattle, only one kilo of meat is obtained.

Similarly, 10 hectares of vegetables directly feed 61 people a day. The same harvest employed as feed for livestock only provides food for two people.

Likewise, one hectare of soybeans produces five kilos of vegetable protein which can feed 70 people a day. The same soybean used for livestock provides 0.5 kilos of meat, the daily ration for just three or four people.

Definitively, the world's current livestock production consumes an amount of food equivalent to the caloric needs of 8.7 billion people, greater than the human population now alive on Earth.

Water, an essential resource for life, is evermore scarce. To obtain one kilo of meat, rice or wheat, 20,000, 454 and 227 liters of water are necessary, respectively. Furthermore, livestock production pollutes water 10 times as much as humans do and three times as much as industry does. Every second, industrial livestock and the meat industry produces 125 tons of waste, polluting rivers and producing toxic gases such as ammonia, methane and carbon dioxide, which damage the ozone layer and contribute to the greenhouse effect. Every year, 300,000 kilometers of forest are cut down to create grazing lands to raise livestock which actively contributes to the desertification of the planet.

It is therefore difficult to understand why so many people who claim to be ecologists and who defend the environment nonetheless often eat meat and other livestock derivatives. In our definition of health, we include the idea of respect for the environment. In addition to notably improving our state of health, respect for the environment contributes to creating a clearly more sustainable economy over time.

We are bombarded daily by advertisements that try to convince us of the magnificent

> “According to FAO, animal feed uses 95% of the world's soybean production and 44% of its grain production.”

benefits of foods and drinks that have been scientifically proven to be bad for our health. The power of the systems that have been established and consolidated over the past century is so great that they have considerably changed humans' diet and, after having been subjected to the same, corrupt recommendations for decades, the general public now has such a false idea of what a truly healthy diet is that it is no wonder that cancer and other chronic diseases have proliferated as much as they have.

Thus, even though most people want to take care of themselves and have the will to do so, they nonetheless consume foods that destroy their health over time.

Worst of all, this erroneous information is so deeply rooted in society that doctors and even parents teach their children to eat these foods, convinced of their benefits. The result is a historically unprecedented degree of overweight and obese citizens, which has a negative effect on their physical, mental and emotional health.

Products made with refined sugar are a particularly good example. In the 1950s, the average person in the United States consumed two kilos of sugar a year, while now a person in that country consumes almost 50 kilos of sugar a year.

The World Health Organization also recognizes the need to establish international regulations concerning the safety and quality of foods and recommends improving the information about and quality of foods aimed at consumers, in addition to avoiding the inappropriate promotion and advertising of foods and non-alcoholic beverages aimed at children.

The aim of this book isn't to examine these socio-economic and political subjects in depth, but even so, I feel I must share with my esteemed readers a minimum of information so that they know that our treatments are not the product of improvisation or commercial interest, but rather of the wise combination, beyond any economic interest, of the best natural therapies, the best possible nutrition for human beings and the best scientific

"The World Health Organization also advises member states to invest in promoting and applying complementary therapies that in many cases are more effective than those provided by allopathic medicine and which are, moreover, much less expensive."

medicine. Our objective is to strengthen the body's cleansing and, therefore, self-healing abilities to recover an optimal state of health, helping us to avoid the use of periodic remedies administered solely in the form of analgesics, anti-inflammatory drugs, antacids, antipyretics, antihistamines, and a never-ending list of etceteras. These drugs are often abused and, even though they may help pass the moment of pain, they commonly have serious side effects that not only don't break bad habits but actually hide the symptoms that make them possible to break and, unfortunately, transform periodic discomfort into chronic problems that generally end up causing much more worrying diseases.

In SHA's few years of existence, we've been through very hard times. The first years demanded enormous effort and because our concept was so different, it was difficult to explain. Generally, we all have the natural tendency to search in the "files" of our brains for comparable information in order to understand what we're being told. Some people thought we were a hotel with a spa, others, a conventional medical clinic and others just a spa. Despite the significant economic losses of those first years, which posed a serious risk to the viability of the project, we always felt encouraged and reaffirmed by the effects that our treatments were able to achieve. People arriving from around the world obtained excellent results and when they told us, marveling about their achievements, it was sufficient encouragement to redouble our efforts; and these guests became our best ambassadors. This is why every year more people trust us with their health and many have even made their recurrent stays at SHA a regular part of their life.

SHA: A NEW PERSPECTIVE ON LIFE

SHA is an international pioneer, a wellness clinic dedicated to improving and extending people's quality of life through the fusion of the most appropriate natural therapies, the healthiest life habits and the best knowledge of traditional medicine. It is an innovative concept that has benefitted thousands of people around the world since its start and has al-

ready won some 50 awards and prizes from the most important institutions in the field.

Those who have visited us at our first location (and, at the moment of publishing this book, our only location), which is located on Spain's Mediterranean coast in Playa del Albir, which belongs to the town of Alfàs del Pi in the Valencian Community, and which faces the lovely bay of Altea, appreciate the attention and service of our dedicated team, the original architecture, the interior design, the spacious settings, gardens, waterfalls, fountains and, most particularly, the marvelous setting in which it is located, an authentic vantage point from which one can contemplate the beautiful scenery of this privileged coast of the Levante, the sea, the mountains, the forest, the valleys and the towns, all infused with pure, clean air, tranquility and an ideal climate. And yet, this is not what attracts the people who visit us, nor what leads a large number of them to return; rather, it is our ability to generate a positive, significant and lasting change in their health and wellbeing, bringing out the best version of themselves.

THE SHA METHOD

Considering the reality we must face, in which, as the years go by, we perceive the slow but inexorable aging and deterioration of our body and, even more so, those of our elders, and in virtue of my personal experience of having prematurely lost some of those closest to me, at SHA our goal is for our guests, after a pleasant stay, to feel more alive, healthier, younger and for their appearance to be greatly improved, for them to leave renewed both inside and out.

To achieve this, we have studied the best life and nutritional habits, the best natural therapies, the most appropriate physical activities for every age and personal condition and, in general, anything that can contribute to strengthening the body's self-curing abilities. In our search, we had the help of many professionals from different backgrounds and areas of expertise, all with vast experience and coming from different countries. Among these collaborators, I would like to single out and honor Michio Kushi, who was president of the World Association of Natural Medicine, advisor to numerous international bodies and considered to be the father of modern macrobiotics. Kushi, the author of nearly 200 books, has dedicated his entire life to the study, research and dissemination of the tight bond between nutrition and health and has been a great and enthusiastic collaborator of SHA from its beginnings.

Additionally, recognizing that we as human beings are body, mind and spirit, SHA has a team of psychologists and psychiatrists, as well as experts in mindfulness, meditation, stress control techniques, cognitive stimulation and rejuvenation and even, at the client's request, we even have experts in spiritual help and guidance. At SHA, we believe in the holistic quality of health because the health of the whole is much more than the health of each individual organ. For this reason, we try not to use palliative therapies that resolve a recurring problem by masking it, we instead prioritize the study of the true origin of any symptom or pathology to introduce the necessary changes in habit and nutrition to recover overall health.

Logically, the SHA medical team, made up of excellent professionals with vast experience, trained in different specialties, contributes enormously to the task of recovering health in all its fullness as well as respecting its holistic quality.

Science has been able to prove that we human beings have the potential to live a bit beyond 120 years, which coincides, with a margin of more or less 10%, with the age of the oldest people on the planet. While it's true that the most important advances in medicine, the discovery of antibiotics, the enormous progress made in surgical techniques and the improvement of hygiene have all contributed to a significant increase in life expectancy, we are still very far below that figure. Today, in the countries with the most longevous populations, the average life expectancy is between 80 and 90 years old; in other words, 30 to 40 years below our natural possibilities, and with, furthermore, a significant drop in our quality of life in the last 10, 20, 30 or 40 years, depending on what our lifestyle has been. To a large extent, this is due to the lack of information at our disposal to adopt the best possible habits to keep healthy and stay alive for many more years. Every time we hurt our bodies with harmful habits, we are making them work harder and this deteriorates our health through the accumulation of toxins, acidification of our blood, oxidation of our cells and so many other destructive processes.

In order to minimize the causes that contribute to premature aging, it's important to start by knowing what our genes have to say. This information will allow us to know what our body's strong and weak points are. We will then be able to understand which habits we must be most careful with and, although it may seem strange, this valuable information can alert us at a given moment to situations that might be normal for most people but which can be harmful for others.

For example, the lack or low production of an enzyme for genetic reasons could complicate the metabolic processing of a food that would normally be healthy for almost everyone but which for a specific individual could cause problems that would be very hard for them to detect on their own. For this reason, we give great importance to this specialty at SHA and have created an anti-aging medicine team made up of expert medical staff who are up-to-date on the latest international advances in addition to the SHA Method itself.

Important scientific advances in genetics can provide us with valuable information about how to live in harmony with our genes. Knowledge about our genes and their environmental-genetic interaction mechanisms helps us in the day-to-day process of feeding ourselves, taking medicine, doing the most appropriate physical exercises, and knowing our own personal ability to cope with stress, which of our organs are most vulnerable, and what the primary risks are that we face are. Telomere length, key to determining biological age and to discovering which supplements can help revert processes of premature aging, along with natural treatments and a specific and personalized diet, help us offer specific programs and treatments that are effective in slowing down the aging process.

> "At SHA, our definition of health is not merely the absence of disease, but rather as a state of complete physical, mental and spiritual wellness in harmony with the environment, an ideal weight, and vitality."

“Corrective exercise is designed to undo all of those muscular imbalances and put those unused muscles back to work.”

At SHA, we pay the greatest attention to this process and all our treatments and therapies are clearly oriented to help our esteemed guests purify, detoxify and reverse any possible damage they may have suffered as a result of bad habits, while trying to create new habits that help them to optimize their health. Another very important part of achieving excellent health is taking part in the right physical activity to help our bodies function correctly and, additionally, maintain correct posture, which is why we have a sizeable team who are experts in a wide range of physical activities. Just by having a look at someone from a certain distance, we are able to guess their approximate age, which is possible thanks to the posture they adopt over time.

The body was designed to act at an optimal level when it's positioned in the correct posture. Unfortunately, over time and through bad habits, we tend to assume incorrect postures, such as slouching, reclining, and even sitting at our desks in all those truly strange positions.

This means that the body hardens in certain areas and becomes soft in others. Muscles become weaker and some may even cease to function entirely. This leads to a variety of health problems, beginning with typical back pains, but which in reality can affect many organs and of course all of the muscle chains.

Doing the proper exercises will help relax muscles that have been hardened and excessively tensed, and those that have had minimal use will be toned up. Basically, one works to obtain the perfect posture for their body so that it functions at its optimal level.

Posture reeducation, yoga, Pilates, weight training (with or without machines), electrostimulation, t'ai chi, Nordic walking, and walks are some of the activities that can help us prevent or reverse these problems.

In addition to breathing – and we can certainly also learn techniques to improve and strengthen its benefits – our most direct relationship with the environment is food. Our health primarily depends on food and we at SHA are convinced that this is the leading factor behind the great results achieved by our guests, thanks to the dedicated work of our team of nutrition experts and chefs who have spent many years studying to learn the marvels that a healthy diet can produce and whose knowledge this book aims to share.

The priority is to recover one's health and once this important goal is achieved, it's only natural that we want to improve our image. For this reason, at SHA we have an aesthetic medicine area that is capable of rejuvenating and improving faces or bodies without surgery, using the latest technologies and advances. In this area, we make use of non-invasive or minimally invasive techniques backed by the most modern technology and medical staff with ample experience and knowledge of the latest scientific breakthroughs.

To complement this, SHA also has state-of-the-art units that provide preventive and medical healthcare services which are equipped with the most up-to-date technological resources and staffed by practitioners with cutting-edge expertise.

In order to make the changes to our guests' health and wellbeing last over time, it's essential to reeducate their habits, making them balanced and healthy. For this reason, at SHA we have created the SHA Academy, which has a calendar of group activities, both physical and intellectual, that allow our visitors to absorb knowledge that they can later apply at home, in order to achieve that positive change of lifestyle and bring the SHA experience home with them.

It's important to understand that to solve health problems, in addition to respecting all of the previously mentioned principles, it's necessary to take each person's bio-physiological characteristics into account, their state of health, the activity they undertake and even the climate where they live: This is the way to optimize their health and energy to the highest degree. The SHA diet takes all these factors into consideration.

The aim of this book is for everyone, whether they have the opportunity to visit us at SHA or not, to benefit from our valuable methodology and this healthy and appealing food. Throughout the book, we will share some of our recipes, fully respecting the principles of healthy food as defined and demonstrated by countless scientific studies, and obeying the strictest recommendations from the World Health Organization and FAO, and keeping with the results of the most recent studies carried out at the world's most prestigious universities.

Alfredo Bataller Parietti
President and Founder

contents

SHA nutrition

SHA nutrition does not consist of a miracle diet but rather of learning how to eat in a healthy way. This will make having to go on a diet unnecessary because it will allow you to permanently maintain your ideal weight, while at the same time helping you avoid health problems so that you can enjoy optimum vitality.

SHA nutrition is inspired by macrobiotics (a term with Greek roots: *macro*, meaning "large," and *bios*, meaning "life") adapted to modern life, giving it a more flexible and attractive focus.

SHA nutrition has been significantly influenced by Mediterranean and Asian nutrition (the Japanese were the first proponents of macrobiotic foods), the two regions that have the longest life expectancy on our planet. This nutrition perfectly complies with World Health Organization recommendations and is line with the conclusions reached by the most rigorous studies from the world's best universities and has no connection to any economic interests nor any suspicious ties to certain industries.

SHA's contribution is the transformation of healthy traditional food, which was considered somewhat monotonous and aesthetically unpleasing, into modern, exquisite impeccably displayed food which takes into consideration the state of health of people in general while adapting the food to achieve the specific goals of each person.

The style of nutrition that SHA proposes is unquestionably a healthy and balanced cuisine without being overly strict. Indeed, the idea is to extract the best and most beneficial aspects of this traditional food and apply it to the needs of each individual, with the aim of helping them live longer and fuller lives. This is achieved through following certain dietary and lifestyle guidelines, given that by improving eating habits and maintaining a less sedentary lifestyle, a balance can be achieved between body and mind that makes it possible to reduce and prevent numerous illnesses. This type of diet takes into consideration not only the biochemical aspect of food, but also its energy. Similarly, it entirely coincides with the purpose for which SHA was created, to enjoy a long life.

FOOD AS MEDICINE

Hippocrates, the father of Western medicine, said, "Let food be thy medicine and medicine be thy food," which shows how important he felt diet was to our health.

Slightly alkaline foods promote and maintain healthy alkaline levels in our blood (pH 7.35), providing our body with greater resistance, allowing us to recover faster from illnesses such as the flu, allergic reactions, colds and sinusitis. Basically, states of health or illness in our bodies are determined by the degree of alkalinity or acidity of our tissues and fluids. A diet based on complex carbohydrates, high in fiber and low in fat, is recommended globally, as much by nutritionists as by health professionals. This type of food amply encompasses these criteria, given that it uses mildly alkaline balanced nutritional components.

In general, the appearance of disease is closely related to the body's degree of acidity, even the massive and steady increase in cases of cancer is largely the result of inadequate diet.

Otto Heinrich Warburg (1883-1970) was awarded the Nobel Prize in Medicine for discovering how cellular fermentation occurs as a result of anaerobic (lack of oxygen) processes. The lack of oxygen in tissues is the beginning to the development of cancer, because an environment without oxygen becomes acidic, and it is in such a setting that cancerous cells appear. According to Dr. Warburg, cancer is primarily the result of an anti-physiological diet and lifestyle.

An anti-physiological diet (a diet based on acid-producing foods and sedentary lifestyle)

creates an acidic environment in our bodies and this, in turn, causes the expulsion of oxygen from cells. Dr. Warburg stated:

- "Lack of oxygen and acidosis are two sides of the same coin: where you have one, you have the other."
- "Acidic substances repel oxygen, whereas alkaline substances attract oxygen."
- "Deprive a cell of its oxygen for 48 hours and it may become cancerous."
- "All normal cells have an absolute requirement for oxygen, but cancer cells can live without oxygen – a rule without exception."
- "Cancerous tissues are acidic tissues, while healthy ones are alkaline tissues."

In his study, *The Metabolism of Tumors in the Body*, Warburg demonstrated that all forms of cancer are characterized by two basic conditions: acidosis and hypoxia (lack of oxygen). He also discovered that cancerous cells are anaerobic (they don't require oxygen) and cannot survive in the presence of high levels of oxygen. Cancerous cells, rather, survive thanks to glucose, in the absence of oxygen. Thus, cancer is nothing but a defense mechanism used by certain cells of the body to continue living in an acidic environment that lacks oxygen. Healthy cells live in an alkaline, oxygenated setting, which allows them to function normally.

Unfortunately, this important crossroads between traditional medicine and what has been taught in oriental medicine for centuries has not been popularized in the medical world nor among the general public. As a result, most people are acidifying their bodies every day, weakening their health and creating the necessary conditions to become seriously ill at some point in their lives, possibly even developing cancer.

No good can come from the permissiveness of regulatory bodies that allow deceptive advertising to equate eating highly acidic foods with healthy qualities. Surely, some day, what happened to tobacco will also happen here and authorities will have to regulate these practices for the good of humanity. Meanwhile, the rise in cancer is alarming and the

repeated warnings by both the World Health Organization and FAO fall on deaf ears.

FOODS THAT ARE PART OF SHA NUTRITION

SHA nutrition is primarily based on grains, legumes, vegetables, fruits, seeds, nuts and seaweed.

Grains: These are mostly the seeds of gramineous plants which have been used since ancient times as a staple food, including: wheat, barley and oats in Europe; rice in Asia; and quinoa, corn and amaranth in Latin America. Buckwheat, rye, spelt, kamut and millet are other examples of grains.

Legumes: These are the seeds of plants belonging to the Leguminosae family. People from the world's oldest regions regularly consume legumes. Legumes are rich in protein, carbohydrates, lipids, fiber, minerals and vitamins. A few examples include adzuki beans, lentils, chickpeas, kidney beans, broad beans and soybeans.

Vegetables: There are many different varieties. They can be eaten raw (in small quantities) or cooked in different ways, such as steamed, boiled, sautéed, fried or in tempura. The vegetables that we eat should be local, seasonal and grown organically.

Fruits: This type of food is noted for its vitamin and water content. Fruit is refreshing and can be eaten several times a week, preferably if local, seasonal and organic.

Seeds and nuts: Seeds and nuts contain less than 50% water. They are a high energy food, rich in fats and proteins, as well as trace elements. Depending on the type of nut, they can also be a good source of vitamins (above all of the B group) and Omega 3 (polyunsaturated) fatty acids.

Seaweed: Seaweed contains high amounts of mineral salts and dietary fiber, a significant protein content and a low total lipid content, giving it the characteristics of a healthy food. Seaweed, the oldest living things on the planet, is also among the few wild vegetables left, which means that it is a real luxury in these times. It is a natural resource that renews itself annually in the sea and is therefore a stable and sustainable source of food.

WHAT ARE THE BENEFITS OF SHA NUTRITION?

Every day at SHA, we are able to observe the multiple benefits derived from this diet. These include:

- More energy, resistance and vitality.
- More stable moods, as a result of balanced blood glucose levels.
- Reduced acidity in the body, which means less inflammation, greater muscular flexibility and a better absorption of nutrients.
- Better digestion by reducing extreme foods.
- A deeper and more regenerative sleep.
- Regular bowel movements.
- Greater mental clarity, better memory and more coordinated physical reflexes.
- Reduced psychological stress.
- Reaching one's ideal weight quickly and healthily and, more importantly, maintaining it.
- Better blood and lymphatic circulation.
- Increased fertility.
- Lower emotional rigidity, greater sensitivity and sincerity.
- A stronger immune system.
- Recovering one's ideal weight, thereby contributing to controlling the global epidemic of obesity.

Obesity is one of today's most visible (and most ignored) public health problems. Paradoxically coexisting with malnutrition, the obesity epidemic is on the rise and is spreading to every corner of our planet. If immediate action isn't taken, millions of people will develop many serious health problems. Within the span of a few years, a country as advanced as the United States has gone from having an obese population of less than 10% to currently more than 35%.

Obesity is a complex condition, with serious psychological and social aspects, which affects virtually all ages and socioeconomic groups and which threatens to invade both developed and undeveloped countries. The obesity epidemic is not restricted to industrial societies of developed countries. Today, world figures show that the increase in the number of people suffering from obesity has reached the alarming figure of 500 million people.

Generally, men more than women tend to be overweight, but among women there are higher rates of obesity. For both, obesity poses a greater risk of suffering from non-communicable diseases related to diet, including diabetes mellitus, cardiovascular disease, hypertension and stroke, in addition to certain forms of cancer. The health consequences associated with obesity range from increased risk of premature death, to serious chronic diseases that reduce the individual's quality of life in general.

The solution lies in educating the public on truly healthy nutrition habits. This is, however, very difficult, because if done well, it would seriously affect the current economic structure of the food sector, from the raw material production stage, i.e., agriculture and livestock, to industrialized food products.

HOW TO EAT HEALTHIER

The Spanish word for health is *salud*, which comes from the Latin *salus*, meaning "integral," "whole." When one is healthy, one experiences a state of wellness and vital fullness.

Malade, the French word for "illness," comes from the Latin word *malactus* meaning "bad habits."

Thus, we could say that one way to stay healthy is to improve one's habits.

Achieving this state of wellness on all levels involves paying attention to many aspects of our lives that we usually ignore. What we eat, what we think, how we move, and how we relate to others directly influences how we feel. Without a doubt, health depends on our ability to relate to the environment, with the understanding that this concept includes the air we breathe, the land we inhabit, the food we eat and our relationship with the other creatures on the planet.

It doesn't matter how much we strive to individually improve any one of these points that are fundamental to our health; if they are not all in harmony, our health will be affected.

Focusing now on one of the easiest things to modify, perhaps because it's the most tangible and the one most popularly associated with health, we need to answer this question: What does it mean to eat healthily?

Simply put, it means giving our bodies the nutrients it needs to work properly and providing it with the energy necessary to undertake balanced physical and mental activity without overloading the organs.

Conventional nutrition considers only the chemical components of food. The holistic concept of healthy food goes beyond that and considers, in addition to its nutrients, its energetic effects, its texture, how it is grown and where it is grown. That is to say, the holistic concept embraces a much more global vision, thanks to which a much broader effect of the food is obtained.

To eat healthily, we need to choose food that is:

- Wholegrain
- Fresh and organic
- Local and seasonal
- Balanced
- Truly food

Wholegrain Food

When we choose to eat wholegrain food, we are consuming the product in its natural state, with all of its nutrients and vital energy. A refined product has lost not only a large amount of its nutrients, but also its vital force. This is what happens when rice is refined: a large part of its vitamins, minerals and fiber disappear, along with its germ, its source of life.

Fresh and Organic Food

When we eat fresh and organic food, we are consuming food with a larger amount of nutrients. Vitamins are lost, among other ways, when food is exposed to the air through oxidation. With every day that passes, food loses vitamins.

Organic food, however, accumulates a much higher amount of vitamins and minerals than non-organic food, in some cases almost double the amount.

Furthermore, organic food contains fewer chemical products, and thus our organs need to work less to eliminate those chemicals.

Local and Seasonal Food

When we buy from our local growers, we are not only helping to promote local agriculture and business, but we are also reducing the impact on the environment caused by transporting products from other areas or countries. When consuming local products, we know that our food is fresh and will give us the most appropriate energy. Nature takes it upon itself to wisely provide us with what we need at the appropriate moment. In winter, seasonal vegetables warm us, and in summer seasonal vegetables are more refreshing and juicy.

Balanced Food

When we talk about balanced food, we are normally referring to the energetic effect they produce in us. Some food has a cooling effect, such as fruit, while others warm us rapidly. Some food tends to produce inflammation and humidity, while others are responsible for contraction and dryness.

Knowing the energetic quality of food helps us select the product that is most appropriate for us at each moment. When we understand the effects that food has on our bodies, we can play and create in our kitchen. We can include a variety of flavors, textures and cooking methods in our dishes that create, through an appropriate combination, the balance our health requires.

Food That Is Truly Food

Nowadays, we call "food" any product we can put in our mouth. However, the real definition of food includes the characteristic of "providing the body with elements for its normal nutrition," and this is where much of the food we commonly eat fails.

Real food is that which in its simplicity provides our body with everything it needs to function correctly.

Our nutrition generally tends to be inadequate and excesses become habitual; we lose the ability to adapt and disease appears.

How can we strengthen that ability to adapt to the constant changes of energy? By listening to our body, by observing the changes happening around us and by learning how to flow with them. Food, directly influenced by energetic changes, is the easiest and most appropriate tool to facilitate that adaptation.

Obesity Trends* Among U.S. Adults

BRFSS 1985

*BMI ≥30, or about 30 lbs overweight for a 5'4" person

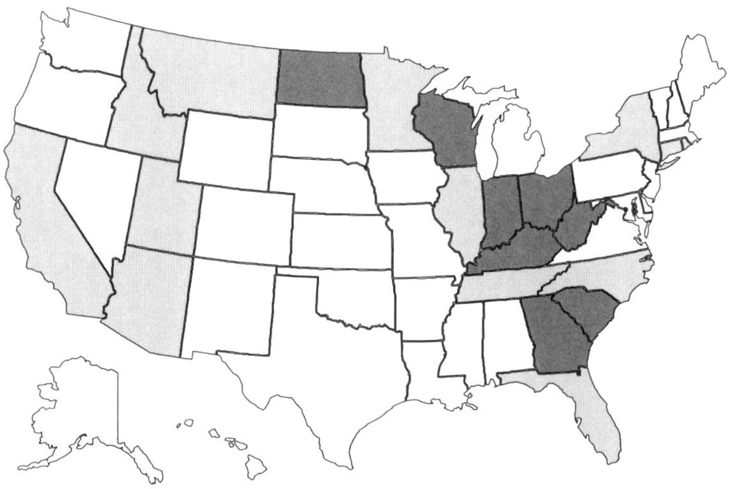

- No Data
- <10%
- 10%–14%

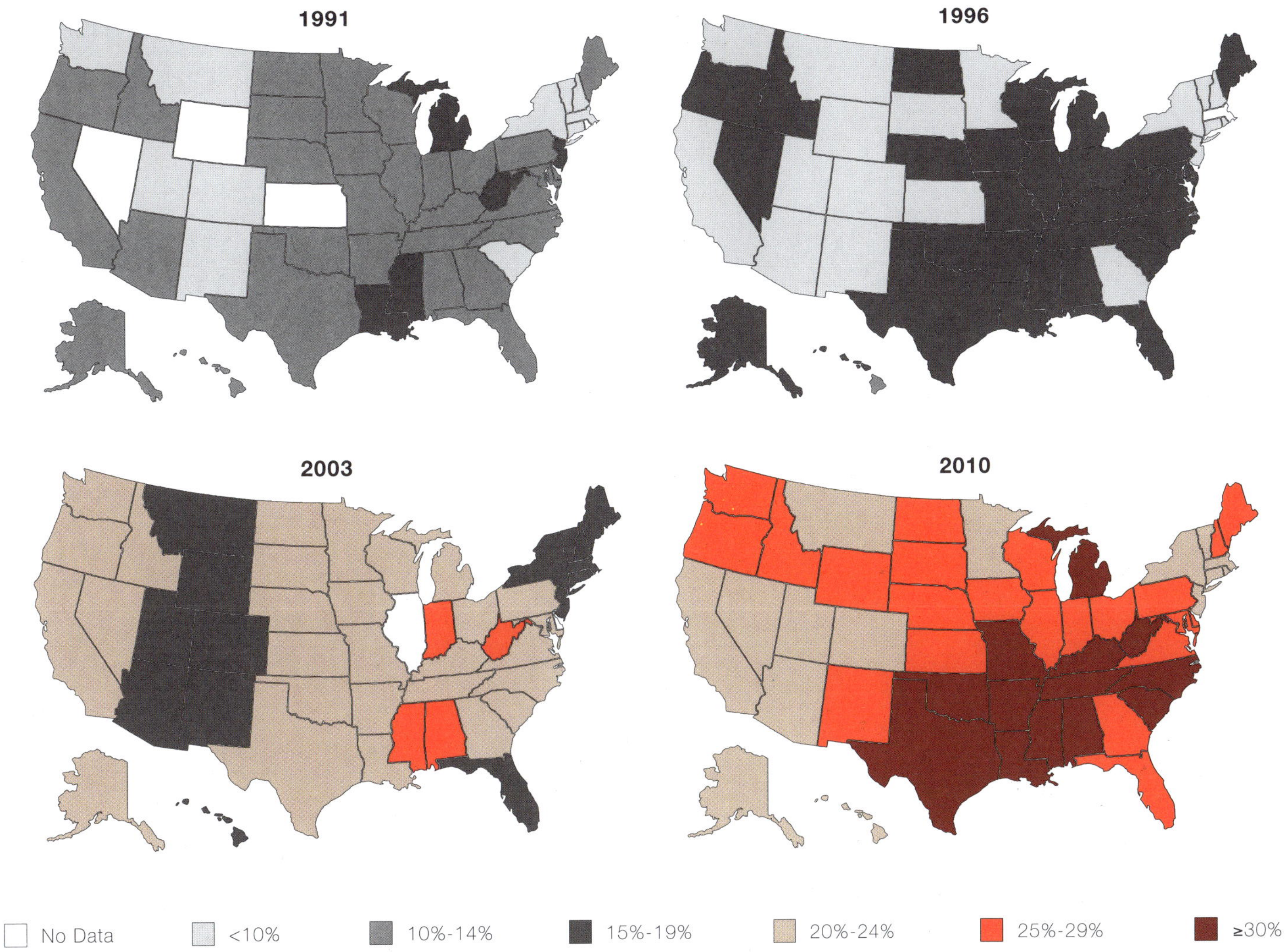
1991
1996
2003
2010
No Data
<10%
10%-14%
15%-19%
20%-24%
25%-29%
≥30%

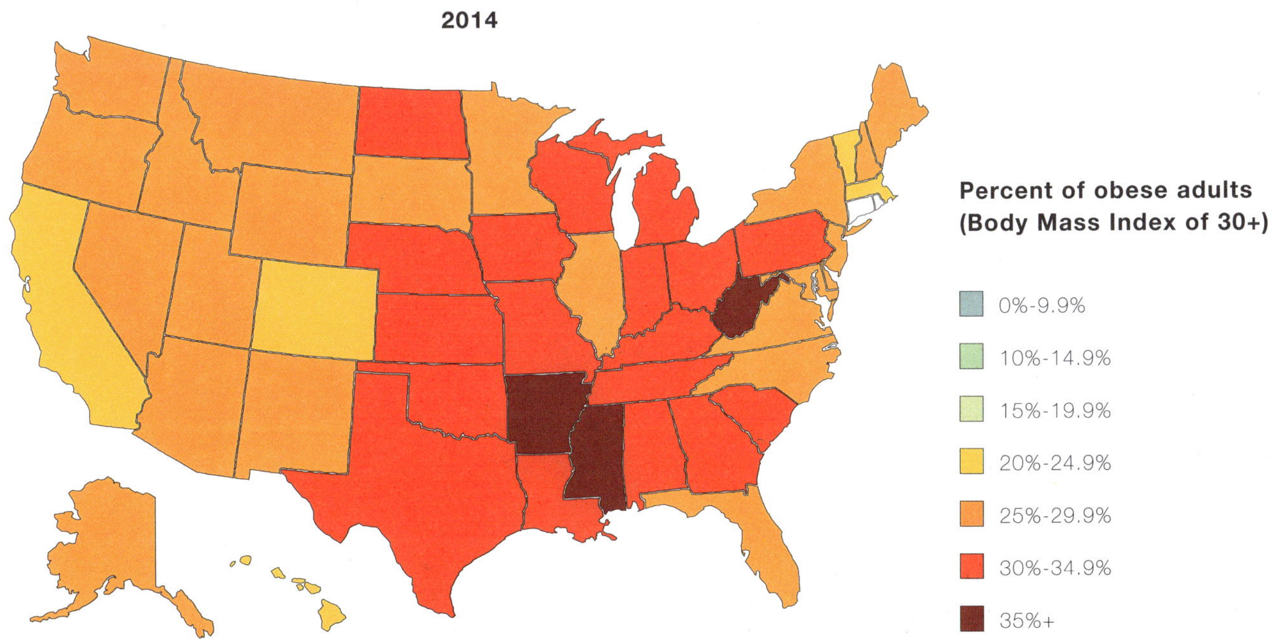
2014
Percent of obese adults
(Body Mass Index of 30+)
0%-9.9%
10%-14.9%
15%-19.9%
20%-24.9%
25%-29.9%
30%-34.9%
35%+

Every season, nature gives us the most appropriate food to balance and tone our body and help energy flow correctly. In winter, for example, root vegetables are harvested, such as carrots, parsnips and turnips, among others. These foods, with slightly contracting and warming energy, help our body to adapt to the cold temperatures of the winter months.

In the summer, however, nature provides us with refreshing foods, rich in water, that open our energy up, helping eliminate body heat and making us feel comfortable and cool in the warmest season of the year. We thus find in our markets cucumbers, melons and watermelons, which grow quickly in just a few months to be ready to fulfill our need to cool down.

If we follow the flow of seasonal energy and use the food that grows around us, respecting seasonal harvests, we will not only have more energy and be healthier, but we will also add much more variety to our dishes.

Spring

The energy that characterizes spring is expansive and ascendant. Spring is the season in which this energy most clearly manifests itself and is a clear reflection of this vibration.

Our body begins to open, to activate itself, leaving behind the withdrawal and calm of winter. We feel ready to cleanse and lighten our accumulated loads.

The extra daylight hours causes our energy levels to rise and all of our energetic channels increase their activity. As the level of subtle energy increases in our body, its need for the dense energy of food is lower, which is why we sometimes lose our appetite.

Spring represents being born again, a new beginning, remaking oneself after the "dead" of winter. Chinese medicine associates spring with infancy, the period of life when we grow the fastest, when we have at our disposal the greatest flow of energy.

The most appropriate foods for this season are those that help us open up and unload what we have accumulated during the cold winter months. Essential vegetables include celery, artichokes, parsley, watercress, the green part of leeks and scallions, asparagus, fungi, mushrooms, radishes, turnips, sprouts, etc.

Cooking methods also change. We will begin to introduce raw or lightly blanched salads, reducing long cooking times and the amount of salt and oil we use.

Summer

The energy of summer represents youth. It is the season of the year in which growth reaches its greatest expansion and afterwards begins to decline.

In nature, summer energy is very different from that of spring, the explosion of vital energy reaches its peak and before settling down. The fields change from the intense colors of spring to ones that are more golden and muted.

Now we need to cool, open and relax our body so we can adapt to the heat without problems. If in the spring we have consumed food appropriate to facilitating the task of cleansing our body, adapting to the heat when summer arrives won't be a problem because we will have rid ourselves of any fats and toxins that we may have accumulated during the winter and we will feel light and full of vitality.

The most attractive foods for summer are those with a cooling, light energy, like cucumbers or zucchini for their refreshing effect. Bitter vegetables are very interesting because they invigorate by activating digestion and circulation: escarole, radicchio, endives, arugula, watercress, lettuce, the leaves of radishes and turnips, dandelions, wild asparagus, etc.

We like to eat refreshing grains such as polenta, cuscus or bulgur, which can be added to salads.

In terms of cooking methods, we will follow the tendency begun in the spring, increasing our intake of raw or lightly cooked food, including juices and grain smoothies for the hottest moments.

Late summer
The term late summer refers to the intermediary period between summer and autumn, from the end of August to mid-October. During this period of the year, summer begins to end, but autumn hasn't yet begun and the weather is often pleasant. The days start to become shorter and cooler.

The energy begins to withdraw, growing calmer and more focused, diminishing in intensity.

This type of energy is present at various times of the year. Between one season and another there is a period of about fifteen days called dojo in which the energy of late summer is active. It is a period of pause during which the energy reorganizes itself.

During this period of the year, we need to center, calm and stabilize our bodies. It's recommended to begin eating less of the food that made up our diet during the summer: cold drinks, raw vegetables, refreshing fruits… and begin to introduce more nutritious and tempered foods that help us strengthen our body.

Yellow, orange and round vegetables are ideal at this moment. These are often vegetables with a sweet natural flavor that nourish and make us stronger, providing us additionally with the calm that helps us flow with the energy of this period: pumpkin, onions, carrots, parsnip, cabbage, celery, turnips, sweet potatoes, etc. Millet, with its characteristic yellowish color, is the most interesting grain for this time of year.

Cooking times will be longer. This is the moment to begin preparing vegetable and legume stews and to incorporate the use of spices that provide warmth, such as cinnamon.

Autumn
The energy of autumn follows the descending tendency begun in late summer, but which now becomes more pronounced. Nature enters a very clear stage of concentration, withdrawal and cooling.

During this time of year, we need to re-mineralize, strengthen and lightly contract the body, restoring the fat and mineral reserves that we lost in the summer months through bathing and the heat, and creating the inner force we will need to face the months of the upcoming winter.

This is the moment to increase our intake of white foods: onions, turnips, daikon, parsnips, cauliflower, white kidney beans, lima beans, pears, etc. The different varieties of cabbages that begin to be harvested during this time are also ideal for this season: broccoli, cabbage, Brussels sprouts, and many others.

We begin to eat hotter dishes and more concentrated foods, without forgetting to add a touch of raw food to provide polarity. These types of dishes will provide nutrients and minerals and will heat and gently contract our body.

Winter
Winter represents the origin, the beginning of the new cycle.

Winter is the season of maximum interiorizing, the most yin period of the year, with very short, cold, wet days.

Energy begins to flow more slowly. In nature, the energetic activity that was previously in the trunk and branches of the trees descends to rest in the roots. Nature withdraws inward, replenishing forces and accumulating reserves for the arrival of spring. This is the moment for hibernation.

Similarly, we also gather ourselves up and need to nourish ourselves with energies that generate more heat. Food during these months is based on hotter and more concentrated dishes and we should avoid raw foods, salads and cold drinks. If we listen to our body, we will notice that we no longer want to eat cooling dishes or drink a lot of liquid, but rather that we want hotter, heartier dishes.

In the winter, one must insist on eating food from the sea, especially seaweed, that is very rich in minerals as well as black foods, such as black sesame, black soybeans, dark seaweed, and miso.

This is the ideal moment to eat vegetables that are more yang, such as roots, which will supply us with fiber and minerals, making them perfect for long and elaborate cooking processes that heat our bodies: onions, turnips, rutabagas, carrots, and parsnips, to mention just a few.

We will also continue to eat green leafy vegetables that provide us with calcium and vitamin C, like cabbage, leeks, parsley, broccoli, Swiss chard...

the chef's secrets

Begin your meal with healthy, nourishing dishes designed to stimulate your palate and internal organs, in a ritual that prepares you for the rest of the meal.

Served in small portions, starters are very important because they set the tone for the dishes that follow. Our starters are prepared with very nutritious ingredients that will also protect your health, such as mochi in a surprising onion cream, or mirin with grilled vegetables.

starters

Seaweed, miso, lotus, seitan and tofu can become the perfect companions of prawns in a gazpacho full of creativity.

In this section, you will find a delicious collection of recipes for all occasions. We invite you to discover them and much more in this cookbook of unique ideas and proposals.

Enjoy!

01

hot cream of onion soup with vegetable paper, crispy mochi and chive oil

SERVES 4 · STARTER · EASY TO PREPARE

INGREDIENTS

For the cream of onion soup
- 800 g dry red onions
- 200 g dry onions
- 300 g white sweet potatoes
- Extra virgin olive oil
- 3 cloves
- 2 bay leaves
- 10 g cardamom
- Unrefined salt

For the vegetable paper
- 200 g zucchini
- 100 g broccoli
- 100 g snow peas
- 30 ml extra virgin olive oil
- Unrefined salt
- Chive oil

For the chive oil
- 20 g fresh chives
- 100 ml virgin olive oil

For the crispy mochi
- Crispy mochi

SERVING THE DISH

Serve the hot cream of onion soup in a deep plate, add some cubes of mochi along with some drops of chive oil. Lastly, slice some long pieces of vegetable paper and stand them up in the soup.

PREPARATION

1 Cream of onion soup
Slice the onions in half and peel, cut into regular pieces and sauté in a medium saucepan with olive oil over high heat for 5 minutes and then lower heat until the onions are caramelized. Peel the sweet potatoes and cut into cubes. Once the onion has caramelized, add the potatoes and a pinch of salt, cook for 5 minutes, cover with water and add the cloves, bay leaf and cardamom. Let cook covered for 30 minutes over low heat. Afterwards, place in Thermomix.

2 Vegetable paper
Slice the zucchini lengthwise, discarding the sides; use a spoon to extract the seeds and also discard. Slice the zucchini into thick slices and set aside. In a medium saucepan add olive oil and sauté the zucchini for 5 minutes; then add the other vegetables, salt and cover with water, cook for 15 minutes over low heat without a lid. Once cooked, blend using the Thermomix and pass through a fine sieve. Place baking paper on a baking tray, cover paper with a thin layer of the purée and place another sheet of baking paper on top. Bake in the oven for 4 hours at 70° C/160° F.

3 Chive oil
Place the chives and oil in the Thermomix, blend for 3 minutes and pass through a fine sieve.

4 Crispy mochi
Cut the mochi into ½ cm-thick cubes and bake at 180° C/350° F for 10 minutes, making sure they are not in contact with one another. Remove from oven and let cool.

SUGGESTIONS

The mochi can be baked with herbs such as thyme or marjoram; add some drops of olive oil to make sure the herbs stick.

This cream can be used as the base sauce to accompany grilled fish by adding chopped chives, miso and a bit of smoked paprika.

scarlet prawn carpaccio, arugula and lamb's lettuce salad with nuts dressed with bergamot vinaigrette

SERVES 4 · STARTER · EASY TO PREPARE

INGREDIENTS

For the carpaccio and salad

- 8 medium scarlet prawns
- 100 g arugula
- 100 g lamb's lettuce
- 20 g almonds
- 20 g hazelnuts
- 20 g walnuts
- 20 g pistachios
- 40 g macadamia nuts

For the bergamot vinaigrette

- 50 ml extra virgin olive oil
- 50 ml Modena vinegar
- 2 drops essence of bergamot oil
- 1 lemon
- 1 orange

Other ingredients

- Maldon salt
- Freshly ground black pepper

PREPARATION

1 Carpaccio

Separate the head from the body of the scarlet prawn, peel and with the help of a skewer remove the viscera pulling from the tail end. Freeze heads for use in other recipes. Spread 40 cm of plastic wrap on the work surface, place two scarlet prawns in the center, so that the tail of one coincides with the head of the other, cover with another layer of plastic wrap of the same size and crush the scarlet prawns using a spatula to make a circle that is 20 mm thick, then place in freezer for 2 hours.

2 Salad

Wash the arugula and lamb's lettuce in abundant water and dry with paper towels. Roast the nuts in the oven for 5 minutes at 180° C/350° F, except for the macadamia nuts, then remove and let cool. Once cool, crush roasted nuts in the Thermomix. Combine the arugula and lamb's lettuce and add the nuts.

3 Bergamot vinaigrette

Place oil in a squeeze bottle, add grated lemon and orange rind and the drops of bergamot oil, shake and let stand for 2 hours. Heat the Modena vinegar in a small saucepan and reduce by ¼, let cool.

SERVING THE DISH

Use a round 32 cm plate, grate the macadamia nuts over the plate, covering it completely. Place salad in a bowl and add reduced vinegar and citric oil, stir well and make a bouquet in the center of the plate. Remove the scarlet prawn carpaccio from the freezer and remove plastic wrap, place carpaccio over the salad and place under the grill until the carpaccio is warm. Finally, add some pepper, Maldon salt and a few drops of lemon juice.

SUGGESTIONS

The cooking time of the carpaccio must be very brief so that it feels like a single dish when eating the salad. If in season, a few rosemary flowers will give the dish a touch of surf and turf.

baked octopus with sake, grilled cabbage and sweet potato *trinxat*, cream of smoked paprika

SERVES 4 · STARTER · MODERATELY DIFFICULT TO PREPARE

INGREDIENTS

For the octopus

- 3 large octopus tentacles
- 300 g red sweet potatoes
- 200 g carrots
- 350 g dry onions
- 400 ml sake
- 10 g La Vera hot paprika
- 100 ml extra virgin olive oil
- Unrefined salt

For the cabbage and sweet potato *trinxat*

- 200 g white sweet potatoes
- 400 g leeks
- 200 g green cabbage
- 50 ml extra virgin olive oil

To serve the dish

- 10 g Maldon salt
- 20 ml extra virgin olive oil

PREPARATION

1 Baked octopus with sake

Rinse the octopus tentacles in abundant water and set aside. Peel the onions, carrots and sweet potatoes and cut into regular pieces. Arrange the octopus tentacles on a baking tray, add the vegetables and pour half the sake and the olive oil over all the ingredients; sprinkle on the paprika, keeping a little for the final presentation of the dish, and add salt. Cover and bake at 200°/400° F C for 45 minutes, remove from oven and remove the cover and bake again for approximately 45 minutes at 180° C/350° F. Add the sake at two separate time. Half an hour before removing the octopus from the oven, turn the tentacles over. Once the cooking time is complete, remove the tentacles and set aside; blend the baked vegetables in the Thermomix and add salt to taste and then pass the mixture through a fine sieve and set aside.

2 Cabbage and sweet potato *trinxat*

Peel the sweet potatoes and boil them in abundant water until they are completely cooked and let them sit in their water. Separate the green section from the leeks and keep for other recipes; cut the white section in half and then cut *à la julienne*. Next, chop up this julienne and set aside. Remove cabbage leaves, cut lengthwise along each side of the hardest section and finely chop the soft sections.

Sauté the leeks in a saucepan with the oil and the cabbage over low heat until well-cooked.

Place the well-drained sweet potatoes in a bowl and mash them with a fork. Add the leeks and cabbage and mix well.

SERVING THE DISH

Heat a non-stick frying pan over high heat, add a bit of olive oil and the previous mix, and fry until achieving a crunchy top layer. Place a 15 cm ring on a round plate and fill it with the *trinxat* to a height of 1 cm. Cut the octopus into 2 cm thick slices and place above the *trinxat*, covering it completely. Lastly, add 6 drops of sake and olive oil sauce and then sprinkle the previously set-aside paprika on top.

fish soup with kayu bread

SERVES 4 · STARTER · EASY TO PREPARE

INGREDIENTS

For the fish stock
- 1 kg fish bones
- 200 g carrots
- 200 g white sweet potatoes
- 400 g green section of leeks
- 2 bay leaves
- 10 g kombu seaweed
- 50 g ginger

For the soup
- 200 g white fish
- 200 g oily fish
- 200 g white section of leeks
- 200 g carrots
- 10 g white peppercorns
- 10 g black peppercorns
- 10 g pink peppercorns
- Unrefined salt
- 30 ml virgin olive oil

Kayu bread
- 2 cups round brown rice
- 6 cups wholegrain spelt flour
- 20 g shiro miso
- 100 g wholegrain pasta
- Olive oil

PREPARATION

1 Fish stock
Peel and cut the carrots into three parts; wash the green section of the leeks in abundant water and cut into three sections; peel the sweet potato and make a shallow cut in the middle to facilitate the release of starch. Heat 2 liters of water over high heat in a pot and when it begins boil, add the vegetables, kombu seaweed, bay leaves and cut and washed ginger. Cook for 5 minutes and then add the fish bones. Continue cooking over moderate heat for 15 minutes more. After this time, pass it through a fine sieve to obtain the fish stock. Set aside.

2 Soup
Remove the fish bones and skin, cut into regular pieces measuring approximately 3 cm x 3 cm. Wash the leeks in abundant water and cut them lengthwise down the middle, cut *à la julienne*. Peel the carrots, cut them in strips and then *à la julienne*. Sauté the vegetables with oil in a saucepan over moderate heat for 10 minutes and add the fish stock, the three types of pepper and salt. Once it begins to boil, add the fish and when it boils again, remove from heat.

3 Kayu bread
Cook the pasta al dente without salt, drain and keep the pasta water in the refrigerator for 3 days. Use the pasta for other recipes. Cook the brown rice in a covered pot over low heat with two parts water for each part rice. Once cooked, add the miso, mix well and leave it in a warm spot for 3 days without mixing it. Keep it covered with plastic wrap so that it ferments. On the third day, add the flour and mix the entire contents, adding the fermented pasta water until achieving a homogenous, clingy dough. Grease bread pans and fill the pans halfway with dough and let sit for 3 hours in a warm spot until the dough doubles in size. Afterwards, place the pans with dough in the oven at 200° C/400° F for approximately 30 minutes. Remove from oven and let cool. Once cool, remove the bread from the pan and cut it into ½ cm-thick slices.

SERVING THE DISH

Place the fish soup in a soup tureen with a lid and accompany it with slices of bread.

cream of pumpkin soup, hake *cocochas*, prawns, citronella mayonnaise, slices of wild asparagus

SERVES 4 · STARTER · MODERATELY DIFFICULT TO PREPARE

INGREDIENTS

For the cream of pumpkin soup

- 500 g pumpkin
- 100 g dry onions
- 5 g black pepper
- 5 g cardamom
- 2 g cinnamon
- 3 g nutmeg
- 1 l oat milk
- Unrefined salt
- Olive oil

For the hake *cocochas* (cheeks)

- 8 hake cheeks
- 20 ml virgin olive oil
- 4 large prawns
- 4 wild asparagus spears
- 3 black peppercorns

For the citronella mayonnaise

- 10 ml soymilk
- 100 ml refined oil
- 50 ml sunflower oil
- 1 lime
- 50 g citronella
- Maldon salt
- Mustard

PREPARATION

1 Cream of pumpkin soup

Peel and cut the pumpkin into regular shaped cubes, cut the onion in half and peel, then cut it into small pieces. Sauté the pumpkin and onion over high heat in a saucepan with olive oil for 5 minutes without covering. Add salt, spices and cover, cook for 15 minutes and stir twice during the cooking time. Afterwards, uncover the pan and add the soymilk, a touch of salt and cook for 10 minutes without covering. Blend it in the Thermomix and then pass it through a fine sieve.

2 Hake *cocochas*, asparagus and prawns

Heat olive oil in a medium saucepan to 70° C/160° F and add dry hake cheeks for 3 minutes. Remove from heat and set aside in the oil. Shave the asparagus using a potato peeler from the tip to the stem. Remove the heads from the prawns and set them aside for other recipes, peel the rest and use a skewer to make an incision in the tail and extract the viscera of the prawns.

3 Citronella mayonnaise

Mix the sunflower oil, the crushed citronella and lime rind in a saucepan and heat to 80° C/175° F, remove, cover and let cool to room temperature; pass through a fine sieve. This is the citronella oil solution.

Put the soymilk and a pinch of salt into a blending cup, introduce the handheld blender into the cup and add just enough citronella oil solution to cover the base of the blender; then, blend the mix without moving the blender and wait for the oil to thicken. Once the oil thickens, add the refined oil while moving the blender up and down. Afterwards, add mustard and salt to taste.

SERVING THE DISH

Pour the very hot cream of pumpkin soup into a deep plate; mark the langoustines on both sides in a very hot frying pan, and place them in the center of the cream. Heat the hake cheeks for a minute in their oil and incorporate them into the plate, having previously placed them on a paper towel.

Add some dabs of mayonnaise to the cream and sauté the asparagus with a bit of oil in a wok. Place the asparagus on the plate as if they were bridges and then sprinkle some Maldon salt over the hake cheeks.

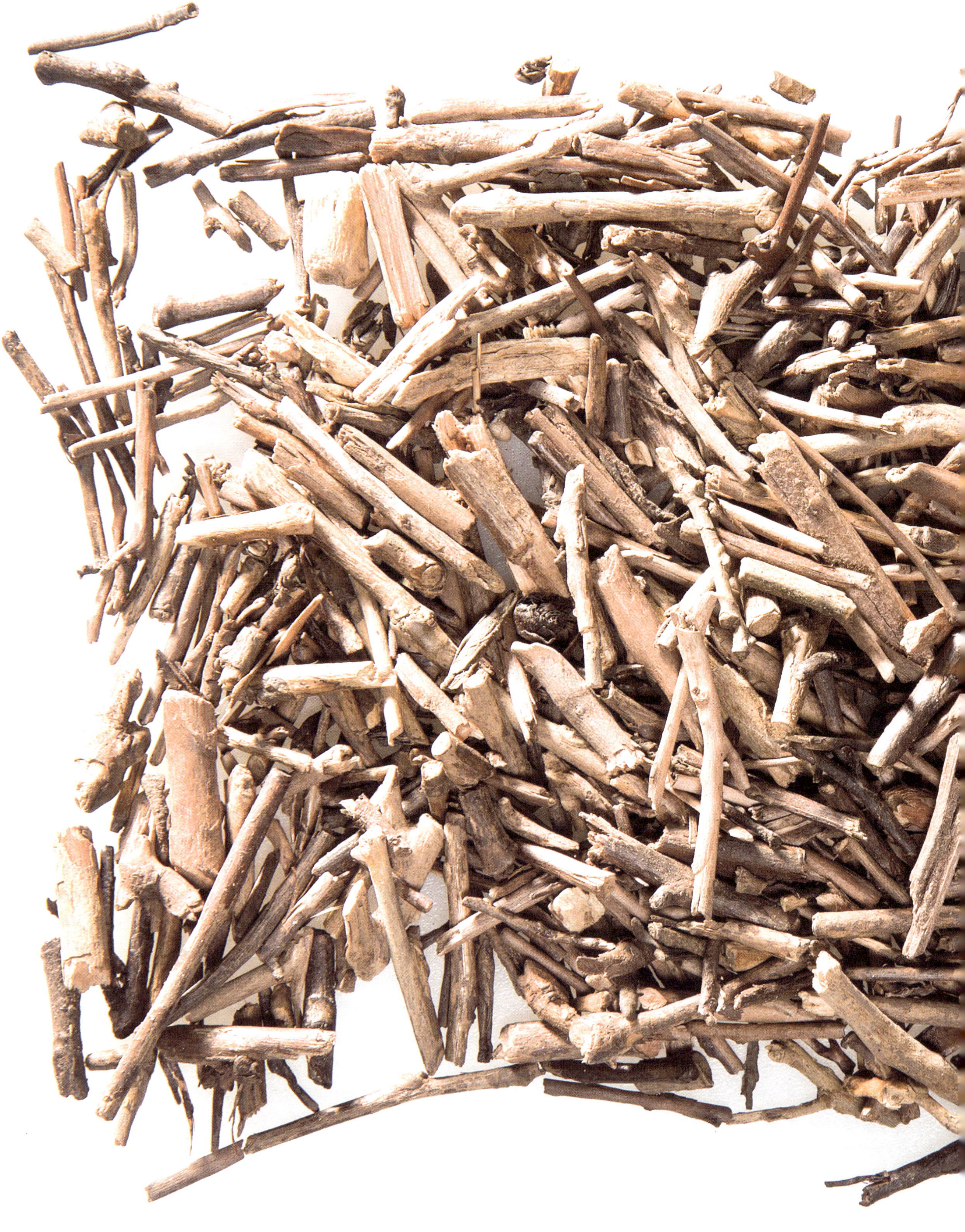

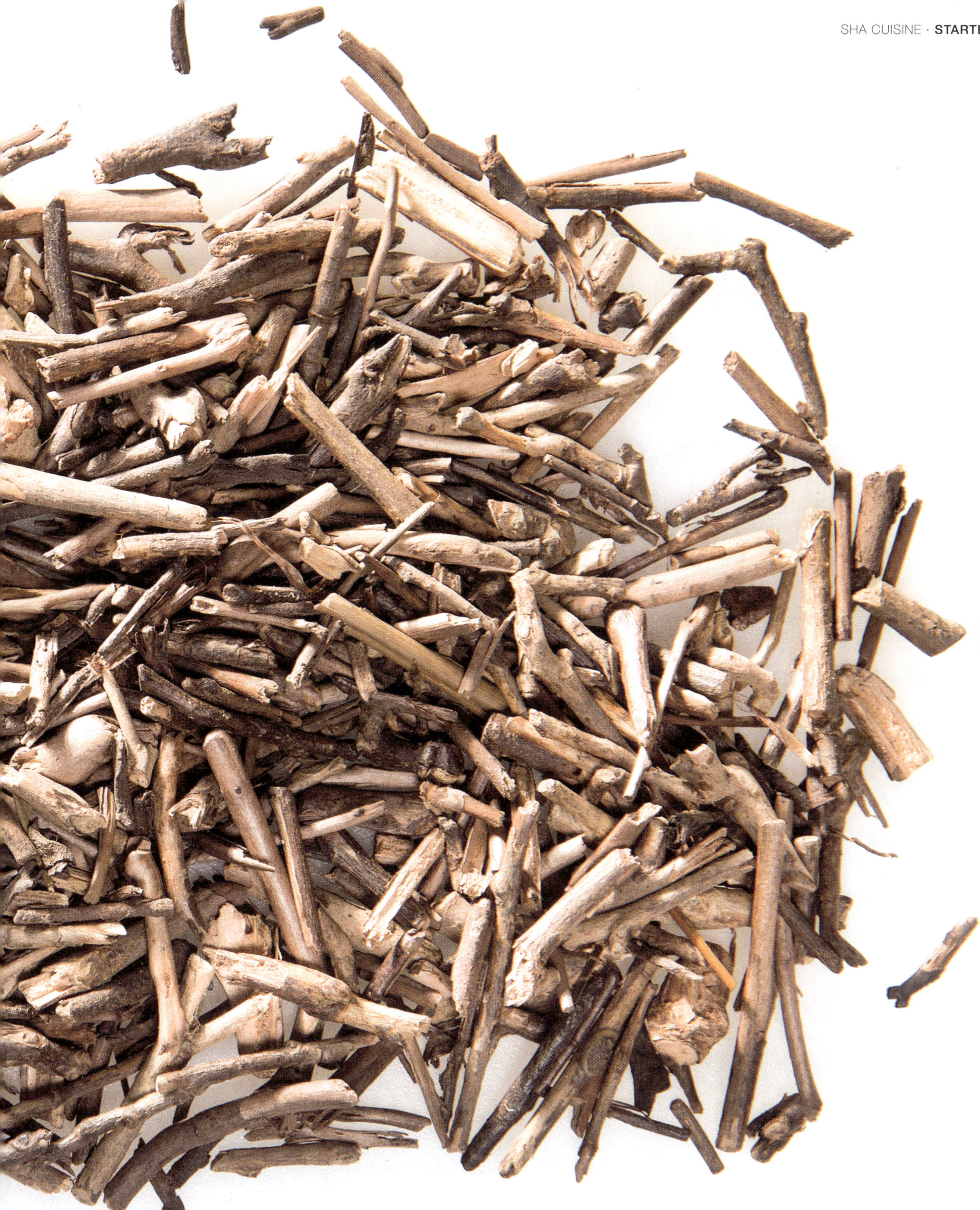

06

smoked mint grilled baby vegetables over a cream of mushrooms, walnuts and mirin reduction

SERVES 4 · STARTER · MODERATELY DIFFICULT TO PREPARE

INGREDIENTS

For the grilled vegetables
- 8 baby carrots
- 4 baby leeks
- 4 red radishes
- 2 small spring onions
- 4 baby beets
- 4 green asparagus spears
- 4 heads bok choy
- 4 small mushrooms
- 8 small broccoli florets
- 200 g salsify
- 100 g red sweet potatoes
- Salt
- Olive oil

For the cream of mushrooms and walnuts
- 100 g fresh boletus mushrooms
- 10 g boletus powder
- 100 g mushrooms
- 200 g king oyster mushrooms
- 120 g dry onions
- 20 ml extra virgin olive oil
- 50 g walnuts
- Salt

For the mirin reduction
- 200 ml mirin sweet rice wine
- 100 g rice syrup

Other elements
- 10 g mint dust
- 1 Aladin food smoker
- 4 glass domes with valves

PREPARATION

1 Grilled vegetables

Wash all the vegetables in abundant water and drain; let dry on paper towels. Remove the green section of the carrots, leaving a small tail to give it a green touch; cut the radishes in half; remove the green section of the onions and cut them in half, removing all layers so that you are left with the smallest interior ones; cut the beets in half; cut the asparagus with a transversal 2 cm cut from the bud, peeling the section of the trunk; cut the base of the bok choy and remove leaves so that you are left with the most attractive ones. Cut the mushrooms in half; peel the salsify with a potato peeler and cut transversally in 6 cm sections; peel the sweet potato and cut into 2 cm x 2 cm cubes.

Boil 5 liters of water in a pot and when it begins to boil, add the vegetables in this

order with a 30-second interval between each: sweet potatoes, salsify, radishes, beets, carrots, leeks, asparagus and broccoli. At this point, add the onion and bok choy for 10 seconds and remove all the vegetables and place them in a recipient with abundant ice water. Keep them in the cold water for 5 minutes and then drain and dry them with paper towels.

Heat some olive oil in a non-stick frying pan and sear the vegetables over high heat on all sides, adding a touch of salt to each of them. Set aside on a tray.

2 Cream of mushrooms and walnuts
Peel and cut the onion in half, dice it thinly and sauté in a medium-sized saucepan with oil; cut the boletus and king oyster mushrooms into regular-sized pieces and add to the saucepan at the moment when the onion begins to become transparent, sautéing the mushrooms for 2 minutes and then adding the boletus powder and walnuts; stir a couple of times and cover with water, then cover the saucepan and let simmer for 15 minutes. Afterwards, blend in the Thermomix to obtain a fine cream, add salt as desired and set aside.

3 Mirin reduction
Place the rice wine and rice syrup in a saucepan and boil until it reduces to half the volume, remove from heat and set aside.

SERVING THE DISH

Place some of the cream in the center of a round 32 cm plate; place the salsify and sweet potato on top of the cream as a base for the rest of the vegetables. Strategically place the rest of the vegetables so that the arrangement is well-structured. Add the mirin reduction and cover the plate with a glass dome. Place the mint dust in the pipette and attach it to the valve on the glass dome. Ignite the dust and fill the glass dome with smoke. Let the smoke accumulate for 20 seconds and then remove the glass dome.

sardines, baked apple, pear compote, caramelized pistachios and baby leaf mix on flatbread

SERVES 4 · STARTER · MODERATELY DIFFICULT TO PREPARE

INGREDIENTS

For the flatbread

- 200 g white spelt flour
- 100 g white sweet potato
- Salt

For the pear compote

- 200 g conference pears
- 10 g fresh rosemary
- 3 black peppercorns
- 50 ml extra virgin olive oil
- 2 ml Modena balsamic vinegar

For the apple mayonnaise

- 100 g grated granny smith apples
- 100 ml soymilk
- 300 ml refined sunflower oil
- 10 g mild mustard
- 5 ml apple concentrate
- Salt

Other elements

- 4 smoked sardines
- 50 g peeled pistachios
- 20 g agave syrup
- 160 g baby leaf mix
- 1 granny smith apple
- 10 g mild mustard

PREPARATION

1 Flatbread

Peel and cook the entire sweet potato in a pot with abundant water and salt until it is completely soft, then remove from heat and let cool, drain and pass it through a food mill. Add flour little by little and knead the mix with your hands until the dough has a certain consistency. Let sit for 1 hour. Afterwards, divide the dough into eight sections and roll into balls; then flatten and stretch them out with a roller to make circles that are 2 ml thick; then use a 16 cm diameter circle pasta cutter to cut the dough and remove any excess dough. Place baking paper on a baking tray and put the circular pieces of dough onto it, then pierce them with a fork all over but not entirely through to the other side; bake in oven at 180° C/350° F until golden brown, turning them over if necessary.

2 Pear compote

Peel the pears and cut them in half, remove the cores with a teaspoon and place the rest in a pot leaving no free space between the pear sections. Add a half a cup of water, rosemary and pepper. Cook over low heat for approximately 30 minutes. Once cooked, drain excess the liquid and remove the rosemary and pepper. Blend in the Thermomix and place the purée in a bowl. Once cool, add olive oil and balsamic vinegar. Put into a squeeze bottle.

3 Apple mayonnaise

Peel the apple and grate it with a coarse grater. Put soymilk and salt into a blender cup, introduce the handheld blender into the cup and add just enough oil to cover the base of the blender. Blend the mix without moving the blender and wait for the oil to thicken, then slowly pour in the rest of the oil while moving the blender up and down. Once all of the oil is added, add the grated apple and continue blending. Lastly, add the mustard, apple concentrate and salt to taste.

4 Caramelized pistachios

Mix the pistachios in a bowl with the agave syrup. Place baking paper on a baking tray and spread the pistachios out so that they do not touch each other. Roast at 180° C/350° F for 12 minutes, turning them over at least three times while roasting. Then remove from oven and let cool.

SERVING THE DISH

Spread apple mayonnaise on a piece of flatbread, add the baby leaf mix so that it covers all of the mayonnaise, add the sardines, cut into three sections. Peel the apple and cut it into small cubes and place them on top of the salad and put a tablespoon of pear compote on top. Add the caramelized pistachios and place another piece of flatbread with mayonnaise on top, covering the baby leaf mix, and grill until lightly golden brown.

On a flat, slate plate, make a circle slightly larger than the flatbread, place the flatbread in the center and garnish the circle with some baby leaves from the leaf mix.

textured artichoke, pine nuts and spelt croutons with shimeji mushrooms

SERVES 4 · STARTER · MODERATELY DIFFICULT TO PREPARE

INGREDIENTS

For the cream of artichoke

- 1.2 kg artichokes
- 75 ml olive oil
- Unrefined salt

For the veil of artichoke

- 400 g artichokes
- 2 g agar-agar
- 1 lemon
- Unrefined salt

For the garnish

- 1 large artichoke
- 40 g pine nuts
- 200 g wholegrain spelt bread
- 100 g brown shimeji mushrooms
- 500 ml virgin olive oil
- 20 ml lemon juice
- Carrot sprouts

PREPARATION

1 Cream of artichoke

Cut off the artichoke stalks and remove the leaves until reaching the whitest section of the artichoke; cut off the remaining green tip section of the artichoke and cut the rest into quarters. Heat some olive oil over low heat in a saucepan and add the artichokes and some salt, sauté for 3 minutes and cover with water.

Cook until soft. Drain and keep a bit of the water; blend the artichokes in the Thermomix and add salt and a bit of the water used to cook the artichokes, if necessary.

Pass through a fine sieve and set aside.

2 Veil of artichoke

Wash the artichokes with abundant running water and submerge them in a pot of water. Once the water begins to boil, cook for approximately 40 minutes over low heat; cut the lemon in half and add to the pot.

Drain and keep the water, adding a pinch of salt. Peel the artichokes until the white section is exposed and throw away the rest. Cut off and discard the tips of the artichokes. Set aside one cooked artichoke. Put 400 ml of the water used to cook the artichokes in a saucepan, add the agar-agar and bring to a boil, add the previously set-aside artichoke and then blend everything in the Thermomix.

Pass through a very fine sieve and spread a thin layer of broth on trays.

Put in the refrigerator for 10 minutes. Remove from the refrigerator and, using a 20 cm circular mold, press to cut the form of a round veil.

3 Garnish

Cut off the artichoke stalk and peel the artichoke until uncovering the first, whiter leaves, cut in half and with a mandoline slicer, cut the halves into very thin slices. Put the slices in cold water with lemon juice.

Once all of the slices are in the water, drain and dry with paper towels. Heat olive oil in a deep pan to 180º C/350º F, add the artichokes and fry until golden brown, remove from oil and dry on a paper towel. Set aside. Toast the pine nuts at 180º C/350º F for 4 minutes. Slice the spelt bread very thinly and toast at 180º C/350º F in the oven for 3 minutes.

Place the shimeji mushrooms in a fine sieve and place the sieve over a flame until the shimejis are golden brown.

SERVING THE DISH

Place the hot cream of artichoke in a deep plate; carefully place the veil of artichoke on top of the cream and randomly add the artichokes, pine nuts, shimeji mushrooms and spelt croutons. Cut the artichokes into eighths and add over the veil. Lastly, add some carrot sprouts.

miso gazpacho with a tofu burger, seitan and prawns with a seaweed curtain

SERVES 4 · STARTER · DIFFICULT TO PREPARE

INGREDIENTS

For the miso gazpacho

- 200 g red peppers
- 200 g green peppers
- 400 g cucumbers
- 100 g scallions
- 30 g dry garlic
- 150 g shiro miso
- 300 g spelt bread
- 200 ml water
- 150 ml extra virgin olive oil
- 20 g salt

For the chive oil

- 80 g fresh chives
- 50 ml extra virgin olive oil

For the prawn burger

- 200 g natural tofu
- 200 g seitan
- 400 g prawns
- 20 g parsley
- 10 g dry garlic
- unrefined salt
- black pepper
- 400 g spelt bread

For the seaweed tempura

- 60 g arrowroot
- 10 g nori seaweed
- 10 g hijiki seaweed
- 10 g kombu seaweed
- 10 g wakame seaweed
- 2 l extra virgin olive oil

For the apple foam

- 200 ml organic apple juice
- 20 g soy lecithin
- 300 ml water

PREPARATION

1 Miso gazpacho

Wash the peppers and cut them in half, remove the seeds and stem; cut each half into four parts and place in a pot with water. Peel the cucumbers and cut in half, remove the seeds with a spoon and cut into four parts. Add the cucumbers to the water with the peppers. Separate the green section from the spring onions and cut in half, peel the first layer and cut into four parts and add them to the other ingredients. Soak the ingredients for an hour and then drain all of the water, add olive oil, bread, salt, water, miso and peeled and sliced garlic. Blend everything in the Thermomix and then pass through a fine sieve. Set aside.

2 Chive oil

Put the olive oil in a blending cup and add the coarsely chopped chives; blend with a handheld blender and then pass through a fine sieve.

3 Prawn burger

Peel and chop the prawns very finely and put in a bowl. Dice the seitan and put it in the bowl as well. Add the tofu and mix the ingredients until uniform, add chopped parsley; peel and chop garlic finely and add to the mix along with salt and pepper. Continue mixing. Make balls the size of ping-pong balls and flatten to form burgers. Cut the spelt bread into 2 cm x 2 cm cubes and toast in the oven for 3 minutes at 180° C/350° F.

4 Seaweed tempura

Boil water in a saucepan and add the seaweeds, cook for 20 minutes and drain. Blend all the seaweeds in the Thermomix and add the arrowroot, continue mixing until the mixture binds and thickens. Load into a pastry sleeve. Heat olive oil in a deep pan to 180° C/350° F, make a small cut in the pastry sleeve and squeeze strings of the seaweed mix to the oil so that it forms a decorative curtain. Remove using a skimmer and dry on paper towels.

5 Apple foam

Put all of the ingredients in a tall recipient and blend using a handheld blender until a foam is created.

SERVING THE DISH

Place the well-chilled gazpacho in a steel bowl, add a cube of bread and on top of that a burger that has previously been cooked in a frying pan with a bit of olive oil. Add the seaweed curtain and some dashes of chive oil. Lastly, add a touch of apple foam.

hot american gelatin, grilled lobster and vegetables with apple foam

SERVES 4 · STARTER · DIFFICULT TO PREPARE

INGREDIENTS

For the hot American gelatin

- 4 lobsters
- 4 scarlet prawns
- 1 bay leaf
- 150 g carrots
- 200 g onions
- 100 ml white wine
- ½ chili pepper
- Unrefined salt
- 100 ml extra virgin olive oil
- 4 g agar-agar

For the grilled vegetables

- 2 medium carrots
- 4 spring garlic shoots
- 300 g daikon radishes
- 1 fennel bulb
- 2 heads bok choy
- Salt

For the apple foam

- 200 ml apple juice
- 1 tablespoon soy lecithin

PREPARATION

1 American gelatin

Pierce the lobster with a metal skewer from top to bottom to keep it straight. Boil abundant water in a pot and when water begins to boil, place lobster in water for 1.5 minutes, remove and put in ice water. Once chilled, remove the lobster's head and peel the rest, being careful to remove the meat from the claws in one piece. Set aside the lobster meat.

Place half of the oil in a saucepan and sauté the peeled and regularly chopped vegetables over low heat for 10 minutes, add the chili pepper and salt and continue sautéing for 2 more minutes, adding the lobster heads and shells. Remove the heads of the scarlet prawns and add them to the dish; save the bodies with shells for other recipes. Continue sautéing for 5 minutes and add the white wine, reduce to ¾ of the volume and add 1 liter of water, let cook until approximately ½ liter of water remains and then blend it in the Thermomix. Pass through a fine sieve and put the liquid in a small pot. Boil the sauce with the agar-agar and stir, adding salt as needed, and then let cool to a warm temperature. Place a layer of the American sauce on a round, slightly deep 32 cm glass plate and leave in the refrigerator for 10 minutes; remove the plate and using a 20 cm ring create a perfect circle; remove the excess sauce. Keep chilled and covered with plastic wrap.

2 Grilled vegetables

Peel the carrots and cut into 7 cm-long sticks; cut one of the points diagonally and leave the other flat as a base; peel the daikon radishes and cut into 2 cm x 2 cm x 4 cm lengths; peel the spring garlic shoots and make a cut where the green section begins; cut off the base of the fennel bulb and separate off sections and cut wide *à la julienne* leaving a pointy end; cut the base of the bok choy and remove leaves to use the central parts. Boil abundant water in a pot and when the water begins to boil, add the daikon radishes and carrots, after 40 seconds add the rest of the ingredients and let cook for another 40 seconds. Cool in ice water and drain and dry on paper towels. Put the rest of the oil in a non-stick frying pan and sear the vegetables on all sides over high heat, adding a bit of salt. Remove from the frying pan and set aside.

3 Apple foam

Put the apple juice in a bowl and add the soy lecithin; blend with an electric blender to create the foam.

4 Lobster

Heat a frying pan over high heat and when hot, add a bit of oil and salt and then the lobster, cut into 3 cm slices; sear the claws as a single piece. Sear on both sides for 30 seconds.

SERVING THE DISH

Remove the glass plate from the refrigerator and remove the plastic wrap. Heat the plate under the grill for 2 minutes and place on the counter. Add the vegetables so that they are well-arranged over the gelatin disc. Add the lobster and, lastly, the apple foam.

The main course is the savory culmination of the meal we began with the starter. Every dish in this collection of recipes has been created with love and has the power to create magical moments at the table.

Discovering how rice can be presented in different ways is a delicious way to express creativity: in a soufflé to brighten up salmon tartar; brown rice to create an innovative paella; and basmati and black rice in a risotto for an exotic touch.

main courses

On this journey into the most sublime flavors, you will learn to use ingredients such as truffles, sake and teriyaki, all of which can enrich a variety of fish dishes like steamed hake in a shiso infusion.

salmon tartar, guacamole and puffed rice noodles

SERVES 4 · MAIN COURSE · EASY TO PREPARE

INGREDIENTS

For the guacamole

- 250 g ripe avocados
- Juice of ½ lemon
- 10 g coriander
- Unrefined salt

For the salmon tartar

- 500 g fresh salmon
- 50 g capers
- 50 g spring onions
- 100 g mustard
- 10 g parsley
- Unrefined salt

For the puffed rice noodles

- 50 g thin rice noodles
- 400 ml extra virgin olive oil
- Unrefined salt

Other elements

- 40 g sprouts

PREPARATION

1 Guacamole

Cut the avocados into two halves, remove the pit and then use a spoon to remove all of the pulp of the avocado. Chop up the coriander and squeeze the juice of half a lemon. Put all of the ingredients in a blending cup and blend until homogenous. Add salt to taste and more lemon if necessary.

2 Salmon tartar

Use a knife to remove the skin of the salmon and tweezers to remove all of the fish bones that are usually located in the upper section of the back. Cut the salmon in the form of the pages of a book, cut into thin strips and then cut these strips again thinly so that the result is all very finely chopped. Drain the capers to remove excess vinegar and chop them very finely. Cut off the green part of the spring onions and remove the first layer and chop finely. Also chop the parsley, removing the thicker sections of the stem. Mix all of the previous ingredients and add mustard and salt; mix well until achieving a homogenous mass and then roll balls weighing approximately 125 g each.

3 Puffed rice

Heat the extra virgin olive oil in a deep pan to 160° C/325° F, add the rice noodles and fry until they grow three times in size. Remove and place on paper towel and add salt.

SERVING THE DISH

Form a teardrop of guacamole on a long plate, add the salmon, previously fried in olive oil for 20 seconds at 180° C/350° F; place the noodles on top of the salmon and garnish the dish with the sprouts.

02

spelt tagliatelle with boletus sauce, asparagus, spring garlic and truffle oil

SERVES 4 · MAIN COURSE · EASY TO PREPARE

INGREDIENTS

For the spelt tagliatelle
- 280 g white spelt flour
- 20 g wholegrain spelt flour
- Water

For the boletus sauce
- 300 g fresh boletus mushrooms
- 150 g dry onions
- 75 g spring garlic
- 100 g asparagus
- 200 ml soy cream
- 50 ml extra virgin olive oil
- Unrefined salt

Other elements
- 5 ml truffle oil

PREPARATION

1 Spelt tagliatelle

Sift the two flours in a fine sieve over a steel bowl, add water bit by bit and knead until achieving a homogenous and compact dough. Flatten and extend the pasta with a rolling pin or pasta roller until it is 1 mm thick, cut the tagliatelle with a pasta cutter and set aside on a tray.

2 Boletus sauce

Wash the boletus mushrooms in abundant water, cut them into ½ cm slices and set aside. Peel the onions and chop finely. Peel the first layer of the spring garlic and remove the greenest part, cut into thin slices. Remove the hardest section of the stalk of the asparagus and cut the rest into thin slices. Sauté the onion in a wok with olive oil until golden, add the asparagus, spring onion and salt and sauté for another 2 minutes, add the boletus mushrooms and cook for 2 minutes, and lastly add the soy cream, pepper and salt, let boil for 1 minute over low heat and then remove.

SERVING THE DISH

Boil the pasta in a pot with abundant water for 4 minutes after the water has begun to boil, drain and add the previously heated sauce, and then the truffle oil and serve on a deep plate.

steamed hake in a shiso infusion, baked carrots and watercress mayonnaise

SERVES 4 · MAIN COURSE · EASY TO PREPARE

INGREDIENTS

For the hake in infusion
- 4 180 g hake fillets
- 10 g purple shiso leaves
- Unrefined salt

For the carrots
- 8 medium carrots
- 8 purple carrots
- 8 parsnips
- 2 medium beets
- 100 ml virgin olive oil
- 10 g fresh rosemary
- 2 oranges
- Salt

For the watercress mayonnaise
- 50 ml soymilk
- 100 ml virgin olive oil
- 200 ml sunflower oil
- 50 g watercress
- Unrefined salt

Other elements
- Atsina cress sprouts

SERVING THE DISH

Remove the shiso from the saucepan and then heat the pan again, bring to a boil, add the hake and lower the heat to cook for approximately 6 minutes, covered. Once the hake is cooked, carefully remove it using a skimmer, place it in the center of a wok style dish and add three dabs of mayonnaise on the sides, place the carrots around it and the Atsina cress sprouts on top of the hake.

PREPARATION

1 Hake in infusion

Fill a low saucepan a little more than halfway with water and salt so that it covers the hake, bring to a boil and add the shiso leaves, remove from heat and let steep for 10 minutes.

With a sharp knife, remove the skin of the hake and check to see if there are any bones, removing them with tweezers.

2 Carrots

Wash the carrots, the parsnips and the beets in abundant running water, rubbing them vigorously, drain and place them on a baking tray.

Add the orange juice, rosemary, olive oil and salt. Mix well and bake at 180° C/350° F for 45 minutes, turning the vegetables over every 15 minutes. Remove from oven and set aside.

3 Watercress mayonnaise

Mix the olive oil, sunflower oil and watercress in a blending cup, blend the mixture with a handheld blender until smooth.

Place the soymilk and salt in a blender cup.

Add just enough watercress oil to cover the base of the blender, blend without moving the blender until the oil thickens, then continue adding oil while moving the blender up and down.

SUGGESTIONS

The dish is apparently simple, but these three preparation steps must be carried out with great care to create an exceptional dish. For an optimal preparation of the hake, the water must be boiling when the fish is put in the water, but not boiling during the cooking process. As for the carrots, it's important that they caramelize with both the orange juice and their own juices.

black noodles with whiting, baby cuttlefish, artichokes and wild asparagus with saffron and soy aioli

SERVES 4 · MAIN COURSE · MODERATELY DIFFICULT TO PREPARE

INGREDIENTS

For the *fumet*

- 2 kg small fish (used to make stock)
- 1 leek
- 200 g carrots
- 1 medium onion
- 2 garlic cloves
- 4 nora peppers
- 30 ml extra virgin olive oil

For the noodles

- 200 g wholegrain fideuá noodles
- 400 g baby cuttlefish
- 1 400 g whiting
- 1 kg large artichokes
- 12 wild asparagus spears
- Unrefined salt
- Sunflower oil
- Olive oil

For the saffron aioli

- 1 clove garlic
- 50 ml soymilk
- 100 ml virgin olive oil
- 200 ml sunflower oil
- 1 g saffron strands
- Unrefined salt

ELABORACIÓN

1 *Fumet*

Cut the leek in half and wash with abundant water, cut the halves into three parts. Peel the carrots and cut them in half. Peel the onion and cut into quarters. Fill a pot with 4 liters of water and, after the water boils, add the vegetables. Cook for 5 minutes and add the whiting. Boil all the ingredients for 20 minutes. Meanwhile, heat a frying pan and add the oil and the garlic. When the garlic is golden, add the regularly cut nora peppers without seeds or stems, sauté the ingredients for 1 minute over low heat and then place in a blending cup and blend. Add the result to the *fumet* 5 minutes before the end of the cooking time. Strain the *fumet* and discard the rest.

2 Noodles

Clean the baby cuttlefish with great care to not rupture the ink sacs, remove the hard inner structure and place the cuttlefish on a tray. Ask your fishmonger to cut the fish for the stock into fillets. Cut into two finger-width pieces and set aside on a tray. Remove the leaves of the artichokes until reaching the white parts, cut the tips off and place the artichokes in a bowl with water and lemon. Cut them in half and then using a mandoline slicer, cut them into very thin slices the thickness of paper. Use the rest of the artichokes for the sauté. In a deep pan, add the sunflower oil and when hot, add the previously drained and dried artichokes; when they begin to turn brown, remove them and place them on paper towels and add some salt. Cut the buds off of the asparagus and cut the remaining parts into slices, discarding the hardest part of the stem.

Heat a paella pan, pour some olive oil in the center and salt around it. Add the asparagus slices and what remains of the artichokes, sauté for 2 minutes and add the baby cuttlefish, sauté for 4 minutes over high heat. Add the *fideuá* noodles and sauté everything until it is mixed, add the stock and boil until the liquid disappears, adding salt as desired halfway through the cooking time. Ten minutes before the liquid disappears, add the pieces of fish and the asparagus tips.

3 Saffron aioli

In a blending cup add the peeled garlic, salt and soymilk; introduce the handheld blender into the cup and add the olive oil until it covers the base of the blender. Blend the mix without moving the blender and wait for the oil to thicken; once it thickens, slowly add the rest of the olive oil and sunflower oil, moving the blender up and down. When the aioli is ready, add the saffron which has previously been toasted on the grill and diluted with a few drops of water.

SERVING THE DISH

Place a 20 cm ring on a round glass plate and fill it with the *fideuá* noodles, smooth it over so that it's uniform, add the whiting, the asparagus tips and the artichoke chips. Lastly, add some dabs of aioli.

swordfish macerated with miso, sake and mirin, purée of cauliflower and red sweet potato, vegetable tempura and sweet rice wine reduction

SERVES 4 · MAIN COURSE · DIFFICULT TO PREPARE

INGREDIENTS

For the macerated swordfish
- 2 swordfish filets, two fingers thick
- 200 g shiro miso
- 50 ml mirin sweet rice wine
- 100 ml sake
- 10 ml ginger juice
- 10 g parsley

For the vegetable purée
- 300 g cauliflower
- 250 g red sweet potatoes
- 100 ml extra virgin olive oil
- unrefined salt

For the vegetable tempura
- 200 g carrots
- 200 g zucchini
- 100 g green cabbage
- 100 g red cabbage
- 300 ml sparkling water
- unrefined salt
- 100 g white spelt flour
- 100 g arrowroot
- 10 g black sesame seeds

For the sweet rice wine reduction
- 200 ml mirin sweet rice wine
- 100 g rice syrup

Other elements
- 1 l sunflower oil

PREPARATION

1 Macerated swordfish
Place the shiro miso, rice wine, ginger juice and sake in a bowl and stir well until the mixture is uniform. Remove the leaves of parsley from the stem and dice the leaves finely and add them to the mixture. Douse the swordfish with this mixture on both sides and place it in a vacuum bag. Completely seal the bag and put it in a steam oven for 1 hour at 70° C/160° F. Afterwards, remove from oven and cool in abundant ice water.

2 Vegetable purée
Peel the sweet potatoes and cut into regular sized pieces; place them in a pot with abundant water and cook over low heat until soft, drain well and purée them in the Thermomix adding half of the oil and salt to taste; add a bit of the cooking water if necessary. Set aside. Boil a pot of water and add the cauliflower which has been previously cut into large, regular sized pieces and cook until you can pierce the pieces with a skewer. Then drain and purée in the Thermomix, adding the rest of the oil and salt to taste. Set aside.

3 Vegetable tempura
Peel the carrots and cut them into 5 cm-long pieces, then cut them into strips and finely *à la julienne*. Cut off the ends of the zucchini and cut into 5 cm-long strips and then finely *à la julienne*. Cut the cabbages *à la julienne* with a mandoline slicer.

Pour the sparkling water into a stainless steel bowl and add the spelt flour, stirring with a whisk and adding the sesame seeds, arrowroot and salt; continue stirring until there are no lumps. Heat some sunflower oil in a deep pan, wait until the oil is hot enough to fry. Meanwhile, add the vegetables to the tempura and coat well. Once the oil is hot enough, add the vegetables in small groupings and fry them until you see that they are crunchy, then remove and dry on paper towels. Make 8 such groupings and set them aside.

4 Mirin rice wine reduction
Pour the rice wine into a small pot with the syrup and reduce to ¾ parts, then let cool.

SERVING THE DISH

Place two spoonfuls of cauliflower and sweet potato purée on a square black slate plate, swiftly dragging the purée with the spoon to form a teardrop. Remove the swordfish from the vacuum bag and cut it into rectangular filets of the same thickness, place in the oven at 200° C/400° F and cook for 4 minutes. Then place the filets strategically on the plate and add the vegetable tempura, having previously heated it in the oven. Finally, use a spoon to pour on some thin drizzles of mirin reduction.

brown rice paella with vegetables and garbanzos

SERVES 4 · MAIN COURSE · EASY TO PREPARE

INGREDIENTS

For the vegetable stock
- 20 g kombu seaweed
- 200 g carrots
- 200 g daikon radishes
- 150 g artichokes
- 300 g leeks
- 50 ml tamari
- 30 g ginger

For the vegetables of the paella
- 100 g carrots
- 50 g sweet potatoes
- 100 g onions
- 50 g broccoli
- 8 asparagus spears
- 100 g cardoons
- 50 g zucchini
- 80 g salsify
- 60 g parsnips
- 50 g daikon radishes
- 100 g cooked garbanzos

For the *salmorreta*
- 30 g nora peppers
- 2 cloves garlic
- 20 ml virgin olive oil

Other elements
- 200 g round brown rice
- 2 g saffron strands
- 100 ml olive oil
- Unrefined salt
- Cooked garbanzos

SUGGESTIONS

The most important part of this dish is the quality of the vegetables and the rate at which they are boiled and then put in cold water so that they stay crunchy and do not lose their nutritional properties. Fungi are very special foods and if they need to be avoided, they can be substituted for a purée of carrots with ginger and cardamom.

PREPARATION

1 Vegetable stock

Peel the carrots and daikon radishes and cut them up; remove the first layers of the artichoke leaves and wash with abundant water, cut in half. Cut the leeks lengthwise and wash them in running water. Wash the ginger and cut it into thick slices. Put all of the vegetables and the kombu seaweed in a large pot which can hold approximately 6 liters and fill with water; boil for 20 minutes adding the tamari at the end. Strain using a sieve and set aside.

2 Vegetables for the paella

Peel the carrots and sweet potatoes and cut them into small cubes; peel and chop the onion; and cut the broccoli into small florets. Cut the zucchini into 2 cm x 2 cm cubes, remove the hardest part of the asparagus stem and slice the tender part, leaving the tips for the finishing touch. Peel the daikon radishes and cut them into cubes; peel the parsnips and cut them lengthwise, remove the middle section and use it for the stock, cut the rest into small cubes; peel the salsify and cut it into 2 cm slices. Peel back the stalks by pulling down from the tips, cut into 3 cm pieces and cut *à la julienne* without fully reaching the end, and submerge them in ice water.

3 Salmorreta

Using your hands, break up the nora peppers into small pieces, discarding the seeds and the stem, and set aside. Crush the garlic without peeling it and heat a frying pan with olive oil over medium heat. When hot, add garlic and fry for 2 minutes and then add the nora peppers, turning them over often to keep them from burning. When the nora peppers are lightly golden, put them in a bowl with 300 ml of vegetable stock from the previous preparation and let sit for 10 minutes so that the nora peppers hydrate and then blend. Add the vegetable stock 10 minutes before completion.

4 Vegetable paella

Cook the rice in a covered saucepan over low heat, using one part rice to two parts water. Once the water is gone, remove from heat. Put olive oil in the center of a paella pan and add salt around it, adding the vegetables except for the cardoons, asparagus tips and salsify. Sauté well and add the rice and the saffron, continue sautéing for a few more minutes and add the cooked garbanzos. Cover with vegetable stock and cook until all the liquid has disappeared, add salt halfway through the cooking process.

SERVING THE DISH

Place the rice in a casserole dish until it is uniformly covered. Add the asparagus that has been lightly boiled in water and salt, the cooked salsify and a few carrot strips. Lastly, remove the cardoons from the cold water and dry them with paper towels and place them on top of the rice.

mackerel, onions and teriyaki sauce

SERVES 4 · MAIN COURSE · DIFFICULT TO PREPARE

INGREDIENTS

For the mackerel
- 4 large mackerel

For the teriyaki sauce
- 200 ml mirin sweet rice wine
- 220 g agave syrup
- 180 ml shoyu soy sauce
- 100 g citronella
- 100 g ginger
- 400 g limes

For the onions
- 600 g dry onions
- 2 spring onions
- 8 French onions
- Unrefined salt
- Olive oil

Other elements
- 12 red currants
- 100 ml extra virgin olive oil

PREPARATION

1 Mackerel

Gut the mackerel and slice them into filets; cut each filet in half lengthwise and just below the bones so that each mackerel produces four filets. Set aside on a tray.

2 Teriyaki sauce

Wash the ginger in abundant water and cut into pieces, blend in the Thermomix and place the ginger in a dishtowel and wring to obtain ginger juice. Crush the citronella and put everything in a pot. Bring to a boil and cook for 5 minutes. Peel the lime with a potato peeler and add the rind to the mix; after 5 minutes, remove from heat and let steep for 15 minutes. Add the mirin, the agave syrup and the shoyu soy sauce.

3 Onions

Cut the onions in half and peel, cut thickly *à la julienne* in the opposite direction of the onion layers and cook in a saucepan with a spoonful of olive oil and the unrefined salt. Cook the onion over low heat, stirring from time to time until caramelized. Separate the green stems from the spring onions and cut lengthwise and then again in half lengthwise so that the onion is in four equal parts. Sauté them gently in a frying pan with a spoonful of olive oil on three sides until they are golden.

Remove from heat and set aside on a tray. Peel the French onions and put them in a small pot, cover them with teriyaki sauce and cook until they are tender.

SERVING THE DISH

Heat some olive oil in a non-stick frying pan over high heat; when pan is hot, add the mackerel on the skinless side, sear both sides of the fish and add some teriyaki sauce; cook the mackerel turning over once in a while being careful not to break the fish. When the sauce begins to caramelize, remove from heat. Place the cooked onions on a rectangular plate forming a wide line and add the mackerel and two pieces of spring onion, two French onions and three red currants. Lastly, pour on some of the sauce used to cook the mackerel.

indian risotto: basmati rice, fruit, vegetables, cardamom, curry and ginger, crispy black rice and coconut foam

SERVES 4 · MAIN COURSE · DIFFICULT TO PREPARE

INGREDIENTS

For the risotto

- 200 g wholegrain basmati rice
- 150 g conference pears
- 100 g golden delicious apples
- 150 g carrots
- 150 g broccoli
- 4 spring garlic shoots
- 5 g curry
- 5 g cardamom
- 10 g grated ginger
- 5 g turmeric
- 2 g grated lemon grass
- 1 bay leaf
- 3 cloves
- 2 g cinnamon bark
- 1 tablespoon apple vinegar
- 5 g fresh coriander
- 200 ml coconut milk
- 300 ml soy cream
- 100 ml vegetable stock (see page 75)
- 100 ml extra virgin olive oil
- Unrefined salt
- 5 g turmeric
- Extra virgin olive oil

For the coconut foam

- 100 g lemon grass
- 250 ml coconut milk
- 30 g limes
- 40 g ginger
- 20 g soy lecithin
- Crispy black rice
- Wild rice

Other elements

- 1 granny smith apple

PREPARATION

1 Wholegrain basmati rice

Cut off the white section of the spring garlic shoots and discard the green section; cut the white section into thin, round slices. Peel the carrots and cut into small cubes and set aside. Cut the broccoli into small florets and set aside. Peel the apple and pear and cut into small cubes and set aside. Sauté the spring garlic shoots, carrots, apple and pear in a saucepan with olive oil for 5 minutes over medium heat and then add the ginger and continue to sauté for 5 more minutes over low heat. Add the rest of the herbs and salt and continue sautéing for 3 more minutes. Add the vinegar and coconut milk and cook for a few minutes. Add the rice which has been previously cooked for 30 minutes in abundant water and lastly add the vegetable stock and the cream and cook until it acquires the appropriate viscosity. Add salt to taste. Heat olive oil in a frying pan to 180º C/350º F and add the rice and fry for 10 seconds, remove and place on a paper towel and add powdered turmeric.

2 Coconut foam

Boil the coconut milk with the lemon grass in a pot. Once it reaches a boil, remove from heat and let cool. Purée the ginger in the Thermomix and extract the juice, straining it through a dishtowel, add the juice to the pot, along with the squeezed lime juice and the soy lecithin. Strain into a tall bowl and whip with a blender to make the foam.

SERVING THE DISH

Using a round mold, create a circle of risotto in the center of a round plate, place the rice crisps on top and add three dabs of foam. Lastly, add some thin slices of granny smith apple *à la julienne* sticking out of the rice.

turbot with white sweet potato and sunchoke parmentier and root skins

SERVES 4 · MAIN COURSE · DIFFICULT TO PREPARE

INGREDIENTS

For the turbot
- 4 180 g filets turbot
- Extra virgin olive oil
- Salt

For the sweet potato and sunchoke parmentier
- 300 g sunchokes
- 400 g white sweet potatoes
- 200 ml extra virgin olive oil

For the root skins
- 100 g salsify
- 200 g carrots
- 200 g parsnips
- Turbot skin
- Sunchoke skin
- 2 l extra virgin olive oil

Other elements
- Unrefined salt

PREPARATION

1 Turbot
Heat an iron frying pan and, once hot, add a bit of oil and salt and the turbot filets with the skin side down; fry until the skin is well done and then turn over; cook the skinless side for 30 seconds and remove from heat. Set turbot aside on a tray with the skin side up.

2 Sweet potato and sunchoke parmentier
Peel the sweet potatoes and boil them in a pot with abundant water until completely soft. Wash the sunchoke with abundant running water and wrap in aluminum foil with a bit of oil and salt. Bake at 180° C/350° F for 45 minutes. Remove from the oven and, when cool, cut in half and remove the entire pulp being careful not to damage the skins. Drain the sweet potatoes and put them in the Thermomix, add the sunchoke pulp and olive oil. Blend and add salt to taste.

3 Skins and roots
Peel the turbot being careful not to damage the skin; heat a frying pan without oil at low heat and add the turbot skins to release as much fat as possible. Remove from heat and set aside on a tray. Wash all the roots well in abundant running water, dry well with paper towels and peel them with a peeler, trying to peel off strips that are as long as possible. Heat oil in a deep pan to 180° C/350° F and add the skins; once fried, remove and wipe away excess oil with paper towels.

Afterwards, fry the sunchoke skins; remove when fried and fold them using tweezers. Dry on paper towels.

SERVING THE DISH

Place the parmentier on a round, black plate, drawing a thick line; bake the turbot for 3 minutes at 200° C /400° F and place it on top of the parmentier. Stick the skins into the parmentier, with the roots in the center. Finish by adding some touches of parmentier towards the front.

The dessert is the final destination of a gastronomic journey and often the most anticipated. Made without simple sugars or dairy products, these desserts are designed to round off a meal and satisfy the craving for sweetness that often comes after eating savory foods.

desserts

We propose a selection of sweet and extravagant flavors, with room for ginger, lemon, apple, pistachios, almonds and cacao in the form of flans, *coulants*, nougats and cakes. A great variety of textures and options to satisfy your desires. Indulge your cravings without fear of gaining weight and turn a meal into a memorable event.

spicy ginger flan, lemon cream, apples with yogurt soup

SERVES 4 · DESSERT · EASY TO PREPARE

INGREDIENTS

For the ginger flan

- 50 g ginger
- 250 ml oat milk
- 250 ml rice milk
- 50 g agave syrup
- 110 g rice syrup
- 4.5 g agar-agar

For the yogurt soup

- 200 ml soy yogurt
- 50 ml soy cream
- 70 g rice syrup

For the lemon cream

- 50 ml lemon juice
- 150 ml soymilk
- 45 g molasses
- 6 g agar-agar
- 30 ml soy cream
- 1 teaspoon turmeric

Other elements

- 2 granny smith apples
- 12 blackberries

PREPARATION

1 Ginger flan

Wash the ginger in abundant water and dry; blend in the Thermomix and filter the juice using a dishtowel. Place all of the ingredients in a saucepan except for the ginger and bring to a boil. Once the mixture begins to boil, add the ginger and boil for 1 minute. Remove from heat and place the mixture in a four finger-deep mold. Cool in the refrigerator for 3 hours and then remove from the mold to cut into 4 x 4 cm cubes.

2 Yogurt soup

Heat the soy cream in a pot over low heat with the rice syrup, remove from heat and add the yogurt. Set aside.

3 Lemon cream

Boil all of the ingredients in a pot except for the lemon juice, without stirring; when the mixture begins to boil, cook for 3 minutes and remove from heat, add the lemon juice and cool in the refrigerator for 3 hours. Remove from the refrigerator and blend in the Thermomix to produce a fine cream.

SERVING THE DISH

Place the yogurt on a shallow, square plate, add three cubes of ginger flan. Cut the apple in half and, with a mandoline slicer, cut three very thin slices and make a cut from the top to the middle and put a slice above each ginger cube and cut the rest of the apple very thinly *à la julienne* and put the strips in the center of the plate. Lastly, garnish with blackberries.

shamadi nougat: sponge cake and toasted almond ice cream, cereal and caramel cream

SERVES 4 · DESSERT · DIFFICULT TO PREPARE

INGREDIENTS

For the cereal cream
- 100 ml soymilk
- 40 g ground cereal
- 10 g kuzu
- 1 g agar-agar
- 200 g almond cream
- 80 g agave syrup

For the caramel cream
- 200 g agave syrup
- 200 ml soymilk
- 250 ml semi-whipped soy cream
- 8 g agar-agar
- 8 g kuzu
- 1 pinch salt

For the almond *grué*
- 150 g crushed almonds
- 130 g agave syrup
- 125 ml water
- Molasses

For the sponge cake
- 30 g margarine
- 50 g natural tofu
- 270 g spelt drink
- 100 g agave syrup
- 120 g roasted almond cream
- 9 g baking powder
- 65 g wholegrain spelt flour
- 140 g white spelt flour

For the almond ice cream
- 60 g soy cream
- 250 ml oat milk
- 25 g rice syrup
- 25 g agave syrup
- 1.5 g agar-agar
- 75 g almond paste
- 65 g wholegrain spelt flour
- 140 g white spelt flour
- Red fruits as garnish

PREPARATION

1 Cereal cream

Heat the soy cream and ground cereal in a pot and once the mixture begins to boil, add the agar-agar and kuzu which has been previously dissolved in a bit of water. Cook for 3 minutes stirring constantly, adding the almond cream for the final minute. Remove from heat and let cool. Place in the refrigerator for 5 hours. Remove from the refrigerator and blend in the Thermomix. Place in a pastry sleeve and keep chilled.

2 Caramel cream

Heat the agave syrup in a pot and once it begins to caramelize, add the soy cream, the kuzu which has previously been dissolved in water, and the agar-agar. Boil for 5 minutes and chill. Refrigerate for 3 hours and then blend in the Thermomix and add the semi-whipped soy cream. Place in a pastry sleeve and set aside.

3 Almond *grué*

Heat the agave and molasses in a pot until the mixture boils. Add the almonds and stir well. Spread the almond *grué* to a thickness of 4 mm on a tray lined with baking paper and bake for 20 minutes at 120° C/250° F. Take out of the oven and use a ring to make circles and then cut these in half.

4 Sponge cake

Put all of the ingredients in the Thermomix and blend at speed 7 for 6 minutes; place the resulting mix on a baking tray that has been previously greased with olive oil, cover and wrap with plastic wrap five times. Bake for 1 hour at 180° C/350° F. Take out of the oven and let chill for 3 hours.

5 Almond ice cream

Put all of the ingredients except for the almond paste in a pot and cook for 5 minutes, remove from heat and add the almond paste, mix well and place in Pacojet cups. Freeze for 5 hours.

SERVING THE DISH

Cut the cake into 5 cm x 2 cm rectangles. On a white plate, form alternating cylinders of cereal and caramel cream, adding the half-disc of almond *grué* and the sponge cake; place a quenelle of ice cream (which has been run through the Pacojet) on top of the sponge cake and stick a chocolate shingle in it, garnish with red fruits.

3

pistachio *coulant*, raspberry ice cream and cocoa shingle

SERVES 4 · DESSERT · MODERATELY DIFFICULT TO PREPARE

INGREDIENTS

For the pistachio *coulant*

- 5 organic eggs
- 65 g white spelt flour
- 175 g molasses
- 65 g organic margarine
- 100 g pistachio paste
- 100 g dark cooking chocolate

For the pistachio crumble

- 35 g pistachios
- 25 g margarine
- 60 g agave syrup
- 1 pinch salt

For the raspberry ice cream

- 100 ml oat milk
- 500 g raspberries
- 7 g agar-agar
- 200 g agave syrup

For the chocolate shingle

- 125 g cooking chocolate
- 100 g rice syrup

PREPARATION

1 Pistachio *coulant*

Melt the chocolate in a double boiler, remove from heat and add the margarine. Whip the eggs together with the molasses at high-speed in a food processor. Once whipped, mix with the pistachio paste very slowly by hand without squeezing. Add the spelt flour and continue mixing by hand slowly without forming lumps. Put the mixture in a pastry sleeve.

2 Pistachio crumble

Put all of the ingredients in the Thermomix and blend until the mix is granulated; place on a baking tray with a Silpat silicone baking mat and bake for 10 minutes at 160°/325° F, moving the mix around every so often during baking.

3 Raspberry ice cream

Boil the oat milk with the agar-agar in a pot stirring constantly, remove from heat and add the raspberries. Blend in the Thermomix, adding the agave syrup. Freeze for 5 hours in a Pacojet cup.

4 Cocoa shingle

Melt the chocolate together with the rice syrup in a double boiler, remove from heat and, when cool enough, place it in a pastry sleeve. Place wax paper on a marble surface and make small chocolate lines with the pastry sleeve so that that they join up leaving spaces between them; add a bit of pistachio crumble in the center and cool.

SERVING THE DISH

Put baking paper on a baking tray then take a steel cylinder that is 4 cm in diameter and line the interior with baking paper. Fill half of the cylinder with the *coulant*. Cook for 6 minutes at 180° C/350° F and then remove from the oven. Carefully raise the cylinder and remove the baking paper making sure not to break the cake. Place the *coulant* on a deep plate with a bit of pistachio crumble, and a quenelle of ice cream above (which has been run through the Pacojet). Place a cocoa shingle in the ice cream and rest the other side of the shingle against the *coulant*.

selection of sorbets and ice cream with neutral spelt crumble

SERVES 4 · DESSERT · MODERATELY DIFFICULT TO PREPARE

INGREDIENTS

For the mu tea ice cream

- 20 ml oat milk
- 2 g salt
- 50 g agave syrup
- 2.5 g agar-agar
- 20 g mu tea
- 50 g white almond paste
- 50 ml soy cream
- 50 g soy yogurt

For the orange sorbet

- 500 ml orange juice
- 50 g agave syrup
- 4 g agar-agar

For the red plum ice cream

- 100 ml oat milk
- 600 g red plums
- 100 g raspberries
- 20 g beets
- 50 g white almond paste
- 6 g agar-agar
- 150 g agave syrup

For the neutral spelt crumble

- 75 g white spelt flour
- 10 g almond flour
- 20 g organic margarine
- 35 g agave syrup
- 1 pinch salt
- 100 g rice syrup

PREPARATION

1 Mu tea ice cream

Bring all of the ingredients to a boil except the yogurt and soy cream. Once the mixture begins to boil, remove from heat, cover and let steep for 15 minutes. Afterwards, strain with a very fine sieve and add the rest of the ingredients. Put this mixture in a Pacojet cup. Freeze for 5 hours.

2 Orange sorbet

Boil 150 ml of the orange juice with the agave syrup and agar-agar, cook for 1 minute and remove from heat, add the rest of the orange juice and in the freezer in Pacojet cups for 5 hours.

3 Red plum ice cream

Boil the oat milk with the agar-agar for 2 minutes, remove from heat and let cool. Peel the beets, boil for 2 minutes and drain. Cut the plums in half and remove the pit. Put all of the ingredients in the Thermomix and blend at maximum speed for 4 minutes. Pass the mix through a fine sieve and freeze for 4 hours in Pacojet cups.

4 Neutral spelt crumble

Mix all of the ingredients in a large bowl, knead by hand until the mix is homogenous and then flatten over a Silpat silicone mat on a baking tray with a rolling pin. Bake at 160° C/325° F and let cool; once cool, blend it in the Thermomix to make the crumble.

SERVING THE DISH

Make three mounds of spelt crumble on an oval plate; run all of the sorbets and ice cream through the Pacojet and form a quenelle with a spoon on top of each mound of crumble.

textured chocolate and apricot cream: cream, ice cream, crumble, twigs, truffles, chocolate crunch and cake

SERVES 4 · DESSERT · DIFFICULT TO PREPARE

INGREDIENTS

For the chocolate cream
- 100 g 80% cocoa cooking chocolate
- 80 g soy cream
- 80 g oat milk
- 5.5 g kuzu
- 25 g agave syrup

For the cocoa and almond cream
- 50 g almond flour
- 50 g organic egg yolks
- 50 g agave syrup
- 70 g organic egg whites
- 5 g white spelt flour
- 6 g pure cocoa powder

For the chocolate truffles
- 75 g soy cream
- 125 g 80% cocoa cooking chocolate
- 50 g pure cocoa

For the chocolate ice cream
- 250 ml oat milk
- 60 ml soy cream
- 75 g agave syrup
- 1.25 g agar-agar powder
- 75 g 80% cocoa cooking chocolate

For the apricot jam
- 50 g sugar-free apricot jam

For the cocoa crumble
- 75 g white spelt flour
- 10 g almond flour
- 25 g organic margarine
- 35 g agave syrup
- 1 pinch salt
- 25 g pure cocoa powder

For the chocolate crunch
- 300 g cooking chocolate

Other elements
- 1 whipped cream siphon
- 2 chargers

PREPARATION

1 Chocolate cream
Bring the soy cream, oat milk and agave syrup to a boil in a pot. Once the mixture begins to boil, add the kuzu (which has previously been dissolved in a bit of cold water to release its properties), add the chocolate in various stages to cut the *ganache* and make it as shiny as possible. Let macerate for 24 hours in the refrigerator.

2 Cacao and almond cream
Put all of the ingredients in the Thermomix for 5 minutes at maximum speed; put the mixture into a whipped cream siphon and let sit for 12 hours.

3 Chocolate truffles
Heat the soy cream in a pot; melt the chocolate in a double boiler. Add the soy cream to the melted chocolate and mix until homogenous. Let sit in refrigerator for 24 hours. Afterwards, remove and roll into small balls and place them on a tray lined with the pure cocoa; coat each ball with the cacao powder and keep them in the refrigerator.

4 Chocolate ice cream
Bring the oat milk, soy cream, agave and agar-agar powder to a boil in a pot; once the mixture begins to boil, lower the heat and cook for 2 minutes, stirring constantly. Remove from heat and add the cooking chocolate. Place in a Pacojet cup for 24 hours.

5 Cocoa crumble
Mix all of the ingredients in a large bowl, knead by hand until the mix is homogenous and then flatten over a Silpat silicone mat on a baking tray with a rolling pin. Bake at 160° C/325° F and let cool; once cool, blend it in the Thermomix to make the crumble.

6 Chocolate crunch
Melt the cooking chocolate in a double boiler and separate two 150 g portions into two bowls. Put one of the portions between two sheets of wax paper, spread with a spatula until it is 1 mm thick and then freeze. Once solidified, break to make irregular-sized pieces; freeze again to preserve.

Put the other 150 g in a pastry sleeve. Squeeze thin lines from the pastry sleeve into a bowl filled with ice water and allow the lines to solidify; 4 hours later, drain the water and keep in the refrigerator.

SERVING THE DISH

Form a line of crumble from one side of a white rectangular plate to the other; put the jam in a pastry sleeve and make a thin line next to the crumble line. Cover the lines with the cocoa cream, add three dabs of chocolate cream and two truffles; place a twig on each of the creams and add a quenelle of ice cream (which has been run through the Pacojet). Lastly, stick a few chocolate shingles into the ice cream.

the recipes and ingredients that heal

NATURAL CLEANSING

The body naturally eliminates toxins through the liver, kidneys, intestines, lungs, lymph nodes and skin. At times, our bodies become saturated and cannot adequately filter out all of the impurities. As a result, you may feel weak, slow or lazy; have skin problems, itching and pain, problems losing weight and digestive problems.

Basically, cleansing refers to cleaning the blood, stimulating the liver and encouraging the elimination of contaminants through the intestines, kidneys and skin. By removing and eliminating toxins and nourishing the body with healthy food, you will be able to enjoy optimal health.

detox

Simple ways to cleanse the body include drinking juices and eating light soups and dishes centered around cleansing vegetables. Be sure to include enough fiber in your meals, from brown rice to organic fruits and vegetables. Beets, radishes, cabbage, broccoli, celery, herbs, ginger, miso, sauerkraut and seaweed can form part of your regular diet while also being excellent cleansing foods.

sengiri daikon and shitake soup

SERVES 4 · DETOX · STARTER · MODERATELY DIFFICULT TO PREPARE

INGREDIENTS

- 100 g sengiri daikon
- 200 g dry onions
- 20 g dehydrated shiitake mushrooms
- 50 ml shoyu soy sauce
- 1 l water
- Parsley

PREPARATION

Soak the daikon and shiitake mushrooms in water for 30 minutes; cut the onions in half and peel. Cut the onions *à la julienne* against the direction of their layers and set aside.

Heat a saucepan and then add the onions and sauté for 2 minutes and then add water and boil for 5 minutes. Drain the shiitake mushrooms and daikon, cut the stems off the shiitake to avoid indigestion and cut the cap thickly *à la julienne*. Add these to the soup along with the well-strained daikon.

Cook for 20 minutes over low heat and add the shoyu soy sauce for the final 2 minutes.

SERVING THE DISH

Serve the soup in a bowl. Add some freshly chopped parsley on top.

sengiri daikon with kombu and vegetables

SERVES 4 · DETOX · STARTER OR BREAKFAST · EASY TO PREPARE

INGREDIENTS

- 40 g kombu
- 100 g sengiri daikon
- 300 g dry onions
- 250 g carrots
- 200 ml water
- 30 ml shoyu soy sauce
- Daikon radish sprouts

PREPARATION

Soak the kombu in water for 10 minutes and then cut into ½ cm strips using scissors and place at the bottom of a pot with the water. Soak the daikon in a bowl for 10 minutes.

Drain and add the daikon as a second layer over the kombu. Cut the onions in half and then *à la julienne*. Peel the carrots and cut them into thin strips and then *à la julienne*. Add the vegetables to the pot as a third layer over the daikon.

Add water and heat; when the water begins to boil, lower the heat to a minimum, add the shoyu soy sauce and cook covered for 30 or 40 minutes until all the water has evaporated.

SERVING THE DISH

Serve in a bowl, forming a tower and adding some daikon radish sprouts.

SUGGESTIONS

Keep an eye on the amount of water remaining in the pot in case you have to add a little more to finish cooking the vegetables.

These vegetables go very well with fish.

03

Virginia cleansing juice

INGREDIENTS

- 500 g carrots
- 500 g golden delicious apples
- 500 g fresh daikon
- 200 g Swiss chard
- 80 g ginger

PREPARATION

Wash the carrots with abundant running water. Wash the apples and cut them in quarters. Wash the daikon and cut it into quarters lengthwise. Wash the Swiss chard submerging it in abundant water and drain. Wash the ginger and cut into regular pieces. Run all of the vegetables through a juicer.

SERVING THE DISH

Serve in a juice glass.

SERVES 4 · DETOX · BREAKFAST DRINK · EASY TO PREPARE

Small changes in your diet can help reduce your cholesterol levels and in turn reduce your risk of cardiovascular disease. It's a good idea to eat foods and dishes that are low in calories and high in fiber. Soluble fiber, such as that found in legumes, oats and barley, acts as a sponge, absorbing cholesterol from the digestive tract. It's important to regularly eat abundant amounts of vegetables, especially celery, radishes and green leafy vegetables. Adding a few drops of lemon to green vegetables can also be beneficial.

lowering cholesterol

Shiitake mushrooms are extremely effective for treating a long list of disorders, including high cholesterol. They are very rich in vitamins and contain enzymes not found in other plants. Shiitake mushrooms also contain a substance called eritadenine that radically reduces cholesterol levels in the blood, and the effect is even greater when the whole mushroom is eaten.

The following recipes are excellent at helping reduce and maintain cholesterol levels. For best results, include these dishes as part of your balanced daily diet in addition to a physical exercise program.

quick pickled pressed salad

SERVES 4 · LOWERING CHOLESTEROL · STARTER · EASY TO PREPARE

INGREDIENTS

- 300 g kale
- 200 g cucumbers
- 200 g celery
- 200 g turnips
- 150 g onions
- 20 g peeled almonds
- 10 g salt
- 20 ml rice vinegar
- 10 ml umeboshi vinegar

PREPARATION

Cut the kale thinly *à la julienne* with a mandoline slicer; peel the cucumber and cut into oblique slices and then thinly *à la julienne*. Use a paring knife to remove the long fibers of the celery, pulling from the bottom part of the celery stalk to the top, then cut *à la julienne*. Peel and cut the turnips in slices and then thinly *à la julienne*. Peel the onion and cut very thinly *à la julienne*.

Put all the vegetables in a bowl and add salt, mix with your hands so that the salt penetrates the vegetables. Place a weight over the vegetables and let it press for 1 hour. Drain and add the vinegars.

SERVING THE DISH

Fill a 4 cm diameter ring with the pressed vegetables, press well and place on a black plate. Remove the ring and grate some almonds on the side of the plate.

SUGGESTIONS

These vegetables can be pressed for 3 to 4 days and thus become pickled, ideal for accompanying any type of protein.

The right amount of salt is very important to prepare this recipe.

02

barley and shiitake soup

SERVES 4 · LOWERING CHOLESTEROL · MAIN COURSE · MODERATELY DIFFICULT TO PREPARE

INGREDIENTS

- 200 g barley
- 20 g dehydrated shiitake mushrooms
- 15 g kombu seaweed
- 250 g dry onions
- 300 g pumpkin
- 20 g umeboshi pasta
- 10 mint leaves

PREPARATION

Soak the barley in abundant water for a day. Cut the onions in half and peel them; cut them thickly *à la julienne* and then cut them in the opposite direction to form onion cubes. Peel the pumpkin and cut cubes that are similar in size to those of the onion. Soak the shiitake mushrooms for 30 minutes. Drain the shiitake mushrooms and cut them thickly *à la julienne*. Cook the barley in a saucepan with twice as much water as barley along with the kombu seaweed for 25 minutes, covered; then uncover and add the onions, shiitake mushrooms and pumpkin. Continue cooking for 15 minutes.

Afterwards, uncover and add the umeboshi pasta.

SERVING THE DISH

Serve in a small casserole dish with a few mint leaves.

hijiki with sautéed vegetables

SERVES 4 · LOWERING CHOLESTEROL · STARTER · EASY TO PREPARE

INGREDIENTS

- 25 g hijiki seaweed
- 700 g dry onions
- 400 g carrots
- 10 ml water
- 10 ml shoyu soy sauce
- 10 ml brown rice vinegar
- Turnip sprouts

PREPARATION

Soak the hijiki in water for 20 minutes.

Cut the onions in half, peel and then cut them thinly *à la julienne*. Peel the carrots and cut them into thin round slices. Boil the water over high heat, add the onions and the carrots and blanche for 4 minutes. Then, reduce the heat and add the hijiki. Simmer covered over low heat for 15 minutes. After 15 minutes, uncover and add the shoyu soy sauce and cook uncovered until all the liquid has evaporated. Lastly, add the rice vinegar.

SERVING THE DISH

Serve the dish lengthwise on a long plate with the turnip sprouts.

shiitake broth with daikon and chopped chives

SERVES 4 · LOWERING CHOLESTEROL · STARTER · EASY TO PREPARE

INGREDIENTS

- 200 g dehydrated shiitake mushrooms
- 600 g daikon
- 50 g fresh chives
- 1.2 l water

PREPARATION

Wash the shiitake mushrooms in abundant running water and then soak them in 600 ml water for one hour; cut the daikon into small cubes.

Drain the shiitake mushrooms and keep the water used to soak them. Put all of the water in a pot and boil, then add the whole shiitakes without the stem.

Cook for 15 minutes and add the daikon cubes. Cook for 10 minutes.

SERVING THE DISH

Serve the soup with the whole shiitake mushrooms and chopped chives in a bowl.

SUGGESTIONS

The flavor of the soup can be changed by adding other types of herbs, such as rosemary, thyme, etc.

losing weight

HEALTHY WEIGHT LOSS

The healthy way to lose weight is to make changes to your diet and lifestyle, which can help you find your natural weight. Crash diets usually lead to weight gain once the diet is over. The key is to eat a diet that is based on vegetables, rich in nutrients and fiber and low in saturated fats. Processed foods contain excessive amounts of sugar, salt and processed fats, ingredients that make it easier to accumulate fat.

Soups are an excellent part of healthy weight-loss programs because they provide us with warmth, they are filling and satisfying, they keep us filled up for longer periods of time and because they are low in calories.

Seaweed plays a vital role in weight loss, cleansing and controlling cellulitis. Seaweed contains minerals and vitamins and is a fantastic way to cleanse the body. It helps normalize blood pressure and digestion and increase energy levels. Seaweed can be added to soups, stews, and grain and/or vegetable dishes. Daikon is another extraordinary super-food that helps us lose weight and cleanse our bodies. It helps digestion, cleans the blood and increases circulation and metabolism. Daikon contains diuretics, decongestants and digestive enzymes. Frequent consumption of daikon can prevent colds, flus, respiratory infections and sore throats. This restorative food is recommended for edemas and helps clean the kidneys and decongest the lungs.

Other foods that can help us lose weight are lemons, shiitake mushrooms, radishes, celery, ginger and pickled vegetables.

It's a good idea to know what you eat, to really pay attention to what you eat, the flavor of each mouthful, how you chew and how much you chew and to choose foods that are both nutritious and pleasing.

The following super-food recipes will help you lose weight and stay slim. Make sure to include them as part of your daily diet.

miso soup with daikon

SERVES 4 · LOSING WEIGHT · STARTER OR BREAKFAST · EASY TO PREPARE

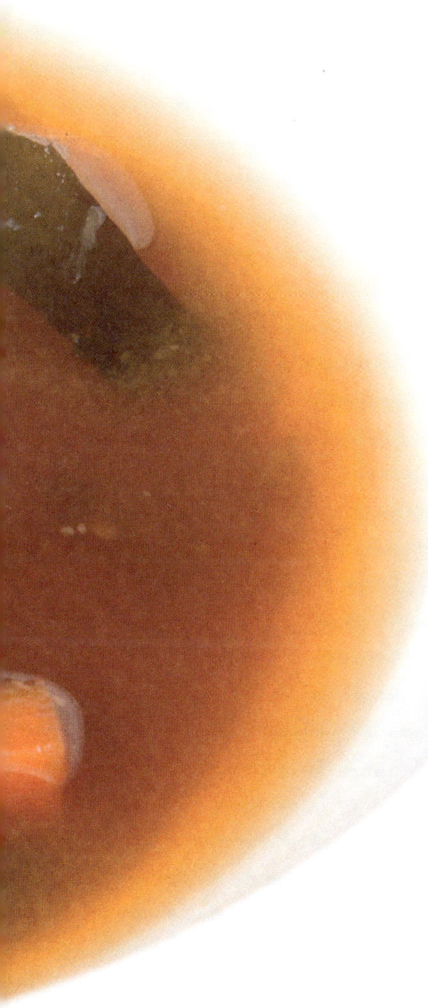

INGREDIENTS

- 200 g daikon radishes
- 200 g carrots
- 200 g onion or leek
- 10 g wakame seaweed
- 100 g mugi miso
- 50 ml water
- 1200 ml water

PREPARATION

Soak the wakame seaweed for 5 minutes. Peel the carrots and cut them in oblique slices. Cut the onion or leek in half and then cut more or less thickly *à la julienne*. Peel the daikon and cut into small cubes.

Place the water used to soak the wakame seaweed in a medium saucepan and add the onions or leek, carrots and turnips. Blanche for 10 minutes over low heat. Add the water and the well-drained wakame seaweed and continue blanching for 5 minutes. After 5 minutes, remove from heat and add the miso which has previously been diluted with a bit of the soup broth.

SERVING THE DISH

Serve in a bowl.

SUGGESTIONS

This soup can be made with other types of vegetables, such as cabbage, bok choy, broccoli, etc. Raw ginger can be added, or some chopped parsley to give it a slightly different flavor.

In order to maintain all of its properties, never boil the miso.

cleansing broth of kombu and sweet vegetables

SERVES 4 · LOSING WEIGHT · STARTER · EASY TO PREPARE

INGREDIENTS

- 30 g kombu seaweed
- 150 g dry onions
- 200 g carrots
- 250 g leeks
- 100 ml shoyu soy sauce
- 1.5 l water

PREPARATION

Cut the onions in half and peel, cut each half into quarters. Peel the carrots and cut them into four sections. Cut the leeks at the line that separates the green section from the whiter section and keep the white parts for other recipes; cut the green section of the leek lengthwise, wash well in abundant water and cut into four sections.

Boil all of the vegetables along with the kombu seaweed for 40 minutes over low heat. Afterwards, add the shoyu soy sauce and cook for 2 more minutes. Strain the broth.

SERVING THE DISH

Serve in soup bowls.

SUGGESTIONS

Ginger juice can be added once the broth is served in the bowl to increase flavor.

The vegetables can be made into a purée with the umeboshi vinegar and used as a pâté.

cucumber and wakame seaweed salad with sesame seeds

SERVES 4 · LOSING WEIGHT · STARTER · EASY TO PREPARE

INGREDIENTS

- 600 g cucumbers
- 30 g wakame seaweed
- 10 g black sesame seeds
- 40 g barley miso
- 1 orange

PREPARATION

Soak the wakame seaweed for 5 minutes and drain. Peel the cucumbers and cut in half; cut the cucumbers thickly *à la julienne* obliquely so that they appear to be half moons. Set aside. Roast the sesame seeds on a baking tray in the oven for 3 minutes at 180° C/350° F, remove and let cool.

Put the sesame seeds in a suribachi mortar and crush coarsely with a surikogi pestle; add the miso (which has previously been dissolved in a bit of hot water) and stir. Squeeze the orange and add the juice to the suribachi, continue stirring until the sauce is homogenous.

SERVING THE DISH

Place the cucumbers in a bowl along with the wakame seaweed, add the sauce from the suribachi and stir so that the cucumber is well-coated. Serve on a black plate forming a tower.

SUGGESTIONS

The aim in this dish is to pickle the cucumber. Another way to quickly pickle the cucumber is to macerate it with a bit of salt and later add a bit of lemon, apple vinegar and a few drops of toasted sesame oil.

04

rice balls with umeboshi plums wrapped in nori, with purée of cauliflower and broccoli

SERVES 4 · LOSING WEIGHT · STARTER · MODERATELY DIFFICULT TO PREPARE

INGREDIENTS

For the rice balls

- 200 g round brown rice
- 40 g umeboshi pasta
- 5 ml rice vinegar
- 3 sheets nori seaweed

For the purée of cauliflower and broccoli

- 300 g cauliflower
- 300 g broccoli
- 20 ml mirin
- 30 g unrefined salt

PREPARATION

1 Bolas de arroz

Cook the rice in a saucepan with two parts water to one part rice over low heat and covered until all the water is absorbed, remove from heat; add the rice vinegar, stirring in zigzag motions. Let cool and form rice balls the size of a ping-pong ball. Once the balls are made, make a cut on one side and insert the umeboshi pasta in the center and close the ball again, pressing it together firmly. Cut the nori seaweed into four pieces using scissors and lightly dampen with a moist cloth, wrap the balls with the nori seaweed and set aside.

2 Purée of cauliflower and broccoli

Cut the broccoli into regular-sized pieces and boil in a pot with abundant water and 15 g salt for 10 minutes, drain and blend the broccoli in the Thermomix, add half the mirin until a very smooth purée is obtained. Repeat the process with the cauliflower.

SERVING THE DISH

Bake the rice balls for 3 minutes at 180° C/350° F and then place three of them on a red, shallow plate; add three dabs of cauliflower purée and three dabs of broccoli purée, and, using a spoon, drag the purée to create small teardrop shapes.

SUGGESTIONS

The degree to which the rice is cooked in this dish is important in order to create a pleasant sensation when eating the balls; when cooking the rice, if you see that the rice hasn't been fully cooked, add a bit more water and cook until done.

Other types of grains can be used, such as millet, to make the balls.

pear and lemon juice kanten

SERVES 4 · LOSING WEIGHT · DESSERT · EASY TO PREPARE

INGREDIENTS

- 1 l natural pear juice
- 1 lemon
- 100 g blueberries
- 100 g red currants
- 100 g blackberries
- 100 g raspberries
- 6 g agar-agar
- 5 edible red rose petals
- 50 g white almond paste
- 10 g agave syrup

PREPARATION

Boil the pear juice with the agar-agar in a pot for 2 minutes and remove from heat. Squeeze the lemon and add the juice to the pot, stir well and let cool without cooling completely. Place the contents in a rectangular mold and place the berries so that they are separated from one another. Place the mold in the refrigerator for 3 hours. Afterwards, remove from the refrigerator and remove from the mold.

Place the almond paste in a bowl with the agave syrup, add two spoonfuls of hot water and whisk the contents.

SERVING THE DISH

Cut the kanten into 1 cm-wide rectangles. Place the rectangles on a glass plate in an interwoven pattern. Add three dabs of the almond sauce and the rose petals which have been cut *à la julienne*.

SUGGESTIONS

This recipe can be made with any type of fruit juice and, in its savory version, with vegetable juice. For the berries to float, keep an eye on the temperature when preparing the juice: the juice must be starting to thicken.

energy boost

To have energy, your diet must be rich in wholegrain cereals and complex carbohydrates. Grains and legumes contain starch (a type of complex carbohydrate) that the body transforms little by little into glucose, which is the molecule the body uses as a source of energy for the brain and nervous system (two of the body's vital systems). To have energy all day long, you have to make intelligent choices about what you eat to feed the body.

There are a number of macrobiotic dishes that can help energize the entire system.

Both the kinpira cooking style and kinpira soup are marvelous ways to improve overall strength and vitality. The kinpira cooking style is similar to a long sauté. Carrots, lotus and burdock root help fortify the blood and are, therefore, good at preventing and curing anemia. Sweet vegetables in kinpira soup are nutritious and are able to transmit resistance.

Millet is a super-cereal that alkalizes and is very easy to digest. It warms you up and gives you long-lasting energy. Millet helps reduce cholesterol levels and can calm your mood. It is also excellent for maintaining a healthy colon. The Hunzas, who live on the slopes of the Himalayas and who make millet the main part of their diet, are known for their excellent health and longevity.

Other high-energy foods are: buckwheat pasta (soba), mochi, seaweed, brown rice, sweet potatoes, legume stews, nuts, miso soup and tempeh.

Juices are an excellent way to introduce fresh fruits and vegetables into your diet, especially if you're not in the habit of eating them. They are nutritiously rich, with lots of micronutrients, vitamins, minerals and enzymes that are easily absorbed by the body.

Juices can be very beneficial to your health when they are part of a balanced diet. They can help you lose weight, increase your energy levels, stimulate your immune system, strengthen your bones, activate your metabolism and nourish your skin. Studies have also shown that juices can reduce the likelihood of cardiovascular disease, cancer and strokes. It's a good idea to drink juices that contain both fruits and vegetables to take advantage of their nutritional properties. It's best to drink fresh juices the same day they are prepared, otherwise the oxidation process will diminish their nutritional benefits.

kinpira soup with dandelion greens and lotus root with miso

SERVES 4 · ENERGY BOOST · STARTER · EASY TO PREPARE

INGREDIENTS

- 400 g carrots
- 150 g fresh lotus root
- 15 g dandelion greens
- 200 g spring onions
- 200 g pumpkin
- 50 g shiro miso
- 50 g mugi miso
- 30 g ginger
- 75 ml water
- 1 pinch salt

PREPARATION

Peel the carrots and cut them into small cubes. Wash the lotus root well and cut into thin slices. Remove the stems from the spring onions and dice very finely, cut the onion in half and cut into small cubes. Peel the pumpkin and cut into cubes the size of the carrots and onions.

Blanche the vegetables in a saucepan with the water and the salt for 10 minutes over low heat. Add the lotus root and diced dandelion greens. Cover with water and cook for 15 minutes over low heat, add the green section of the diced spring onions for the last 2 minutes of the cooking time. Remove from heat and add the two types of miso which have previously been diluted with a bit of the broth. Purée the ginger in the Thermomix and add the resulting juice to the soup.

SERVING THE DISH

Serve the soup in an elongated bowl with three slices of lotus root and garnished with a few dandelion greens.

SUGGESTIONS

This soup is made with sweet vegetables; to add a fresh touch, use a bit of fennel.

If the lotus root is dehydrated, it should be soaked for 10 minutes in water before using.

carrot and dandelion greens kinpira

SERVES 4 · ENERGY BOOST · STARTER · EASY TO PREPARE

INGREDIENTS

- 80 g dandelion greens
- 300 g carrots
- 30 ml mirin
- 10 ml water
- 20 ml shoyu soy sauce
- 20 g ginger

PREPARATION

Peel the carrots and cut into diagonal slices and then cut into strips. Heat the mirin and the water in a pot and add the carrots and dandelion greens and cook very quickly over medium heat for 5 minutes, then add the ginger and shoyu soy sauce and continue cooking until the liquids are completely reduced.

SERVING THE DISH

Serve in an elongated plate with a few dandelion greens.

SUGGESTIONS

Kinpira can be made with several types of vegetables, but the procedure is the same.

It is essential to control the heat to ensure the beneficial properties of this recipe are not lost.

03

sautéed hijiki, carrots and onions with tempeh and fresh ginger

SERVES 4 · ENERGY BOOST · MAIN COURSE · MODERATELY DIFFICULT TO PREPARE

INGREDIENTS

- 150 g hijiki seaweed
- 30 ml water
- 10 ml lemon juice
- 5 g apple concentrate
- 200 g spring onions
- 300 g carrots
- 600 g tempeh
- 100 ml shoyu soy sauce
- 100 g ginger
- 30 g parsley
- Cucumber sprouts

PREPARATION

Soak the hijiki for 15 minutes and then drain. Cut the tempeh into cubes and boil in water with 30 ml of shoyu soy sauce for 15 minutes, then drain. Peel the carrots and cut into small cubes; separate the green part of the spring onions and set aside; peel off a layer of the onion and cut into small cubes. Heat the water in a saucepan and add the onions and carrots and cook for 5 minutes over medium heat, move the vegetables to one side and roast the tempeh, move the tempeh to one side of the saucepan with the vegetables and add the hijiki. Layer the vegetables over the hijiki and the tempeh. Add water until half of the hijiki is covered. Cover and cook for 15 minutes at low heat. Then uncover and add the rest of the shoyu soy sauce, the lemon juice, apple concentrate, parsley and juice from the ginger. Dice the green section of the spring onions very finely and add to the dish. Continue cooking and stirring the entire dish for 5 minutes and then remove from heat.

SERVING THE DISH

Serve in a small casserole dish with a few cucumber sprouts.

SUGGESTIONS

Seitan can be used instead of tempeh. To change the tempeh's special flavor, boil it in vegetable stock or add various types of herbs.

04

millet with cauliflower, red endives and watercress

SERVES 4 · ENERGY BOOST · MAIN COURSE · EASY TO PREPARE

INGREDIENTS

- 200 g millet
- 600 g cauliflower
- 2 endives
- 2 leaves watercress
- 20 g salt
- 10 ml water
- 5 g nutmeg

PREPARATION

Cut the cauliflower into regular-sized pieces and blanche in the boiling water in a saucepan for 5 minutes then add the millet (three parts water to one part millet). Once the mixture begins to boil, add the nutmeg and the salt. Cook covered for approximately 30 minutes. Remove from heat.

SERVING THE DISH

Using a mold, arrange the millet on an oval plate, add the endives around it and top with some watercress.

drinks and juices

In this section, you will discover delicious juices and drinks with which to enjoy pleasant moments, alone or with others, and stay healthy at the same time. Natural juices and detox drinks are a delicious and healthy way to cleanse and detoxify the body. Their water and nutrient content makes our healthy drinks the perfect ally to help us stay hydrated, notwithstanding water.

Presented in a pleasing way, these drinks are a delight to the eye and palette and are sure to provide us with unique moments. **TO YOUR HEALTH!**

01

SHA sunrise

SERVES 4 · DRINKS AND JUICES · COCKTAIL · EASY TO PREPARE

INGREDIENTS

- 550 g carrots
- 280 g granny smith apples
- 40 g granny smith apples for garnish

PREPARATION

Peel the carrots, wash the apples and cut them into quarters. Set aside 40 g of apples. Make a carrot and apple juice in the juicer. Strain with a fine sieve.

Cut the remaining 40 g of apple into 4 mm thick slices and then *à la julienne* so that the skin remains on the tips.

SERVING THE COCKTAIL

Pour the juice into a wineglass and place the apple strips on top in the shape of a square.

SHA detox

SERVES 4 · DRINKS AND JUICES · COCKTAIL · EASY TO PREPARE

INGREDIENTS

- 200 g Swiss chard
- 50 g daikon radishes
- 240 g carrots
- 200 g golden delicious apples

PREPARATION

Cut the leaves from the stems of the Swiss chard, wash the leaves submerging them in abundant water and rubbing them against each other, drain and wash again, this time removing the chard from the water by hand so that any dirt remains at the bottom of the water. Wash the daikon radishes and carrots in running water and cut in half. Wash the apples and cut them into quarters.

Run all of the vegetables through a juicer.

SERVING THE COCKTAIL

Serve the juice in a low glass with a slice of fresh daikon.

03

muteani

SERVES 4 · DRINKS AND JUICES · COCKTAIL · EASY TO PREPARE

INGREDIENTS

- 15 g mu tea
- 1 lemon
- 1 green olive

PREPARATION

Boil two cups of water in a pot and when the water begins to boil, add the mu tea, remove from heat, let steep for 10 minutes and then cool in the refrigerator. Wash the lemon in abundant water and cut into thin slices.

SERVING THE COCKTAIL

Pour the mu tea into a cocktail glass. Add a slice of lemon. Pierce the olive with a toothpick and place it in the drink.

SHA red velvet

SERVES 4 · DRINKS AND JUICES · COCKTAIL · EASY TO PREPARE

INGREDIENTS

- 900 g watermelon
- 80 g strawberries

PREPARATION

Completely submerge the strawberries in a bowl of water, carefully stir the strawberries by hand and then drain. Cut the crown (the green part) off the strawberries and discard. Blend the strawberries in a blender and then strain through a fine sieve.

Peel the watermelon and cut into regular-sized pieces and run through a juicer; set aside.

SERVING THE COCKTAIL

Mix the watermelon juice and strawberry purée in a glass or bowl, stir well and serve in a cocktail glass. Add some slices of strawberry as garnish.

SHA exclusivitea

SERVES 4 · DRINKS AND JUICES · COCKTAIL · EASY TO PREPARE

INGREDIENTS

- 15 g kukicha tea
- 1 sprig rosemary
- 1 orange
- Water

PREPARATION

Boil the kukicha tea in a small pot with a cup and a half of water, let boil for 3 minutes over low heat and then remove from heat. Add the rosemary and cover, let steep for 5 minutes and then chill.

Cut the orange into thin slices.

SERVING THE COCKTAIL

Serve the tea in a cocktail glass and add the orange slices. Garnish with a small sprig of rosemary.

mu-jito

SERVES 4 · DRINKS AND JUICES · COCKTAIL · EASY TO PREPARE

INGREDIENTS

- 20 g mu tea
- 200 ml water
- 20 g rice syrup
- 3 sprigs mint
- Crushed ice
- 1 lime

PREPARATION

Boil water in a pot, add the tea and syrup, remove from heat and let steep for 10 minutes and then chill in the refrigerator. Wash the lime with abundant water and cut into quarters.

Put the crushed ice in a cocktail shaker with two lime quarters and the mu tea infusion, add the lightly chopped mint, saving a few small leaves as garnish, shake.

SERVING THE COCKTAIL

Pour the tea into a tall cocktail glass and add the lime quarters. Garnish with a few mint leaves.

a tour of the world's gastronomy

On this long path in search of healthy cuisine, we have traveled the world and become familiar with the most varied cultures, a wide range of gastronomies and, above all, people. A culinary recipe is a process whereby several properly combined and prepared ingredients create something whose whole is more than the sum of its parts. Our obsession, however, isn't limited to producing the best dishes; our obsession is HEALTH. We use food to preserve health and even to recover it.

"Let food be thy medicine and medicine thy food," said Hippocrates.

We have met people on this path who have passionately dedicated their lives to healthy food.

In honor of these special people, we have gathered a selection of the best chefs who give soul to food, not only to delight your palette, but also to bring health to your table.

Jadranka Boban Pejić is the leading name in natural foodism in Croatia. She became a professor of macrobiotics at the Kushi Institute of Boston. Over the past twenty years, she has led numerous educational programs. She is the author of numerous articles and regularly collaborates with several newspapers and magazines, as well as television shows. With her husband, Zlatko, she founded the Makronova Institute in Zagreb where she created and leads the School of Natural Cooking program and the concept of Comprehensive Women's Health. Along with her husband, she has taught many courses in the most important cities in Croatia and abroad. In her work, Boban Pejić often combines her experience in special education and macrobiotics, especially when working with parents and children.

Boban Pejić is the author of several books: *Natural and Sweet*, *For Babies and Kids*, *I Cook and Eat Healthy*, *Grains*, *Algae*, *Spring*, *Summer and Winter* and is the coauthor of the book, *Food for Life*. She won the prestigious international Gourmand World Cookbook Award in 2007for her book *Summer* in the category of Best Vegetarian Cookbook in the World.

Boban Pejić is also the executive director of the Biovega Company, a leading promoter of organic products in Croatia, in addition to being a retailer of certified organic products through the bio&bio chain of health food stores.

Sweet potato pancakes

The sweet potato, high in nutrients, is a tuber with few similarities to the potato. Sweet potatoes are grown in Croatia and are sold almost everywhere.

INGREDIENTS

- 1 ½ cups wheat flour 850 type (ideal for bread)
- 1 ½ teaspoons baking powder
- ½ teaspoon salt
- 1 ½ cups oat milk
- 1 cup sweet potato purée
- 2 tablespoons chopped parsley
- 1 pinch white pepper
- 6 tablespoons oat cream
- 2 tablespoons olive oil

PREPARATION

Mix all of the ingredients together and prepare a thick pancake batter.
Heat oil in a frying pan and add the batter when the pan is hot. Because the batter is too thick to spread by itself, spread with a spatula.
Flip the pancake so that it cooks on both sides.

Recipes from the cookbook *Summer*, published by Planetopija, Zagreb, Croatia.
Photo credit: Dag Oršić

NOTE

These pancakes are delicious on their own but can also be enjoyed with different ingredients such as tofu or cream of peas. Served with a cream as a spread and steamed vegetables, they make a complete meal. Sweet potato pancakes are delicious when served with salad.

Delicious smoothie

A fresh, fragrant and delicious summer passion

INGREDIENTS

- ½ cup amaranth
- 1 ½ cups apple juice
- Orange zest
- ½ teaspoon vanilla powder
- 2 ½ cups raspberries
- 2 tablespoons rice syrup
- 100 ml oat cream
- ½ cup sliced almonds

PREPARATION

Boil the apple juice and add the amaranth. Cook covered over low heat for 10 minutes.

Add the vanilla powder and orange zest and cook for another 10 minutes.

Add the rice syrup, raspberries and oat milk; beat the ingredients until the mixture is smooth. Garnish with roasted sliced almonds.

Country fig and peach pie

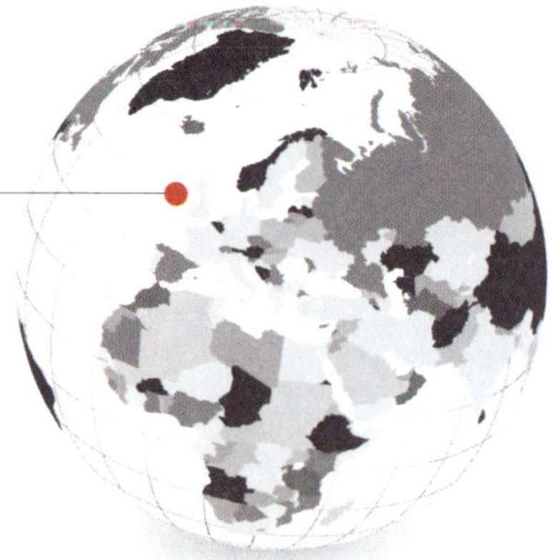

Aine McAteer's relationship with macrobiotics began in her native Ireland more than 35 years ago. After working for two years at Ireland's first macrobiotic restaurant, where she experienced dramatic improvements in her health and wellbeing, McAteer continued her path, searching for teachers in the United Kingdom and the United States. She has studied with the best international macrobiotic teachers and her career as a personal chef has taken her around the world and into the lives of many people, including top Hollywood actors, athletes and iconic musicians.

McAteer has often traveled with her clients and has had the opportunity to explore the cuisines of other cultures, which has given her greater creativity in her cooking style. McAteer's first cookbook, *Recipes to Nurture*, won the Gourmand World Cookbook award in 2005 for "Best Health and Nutrition Cookbook in the World." She has also published two more books in Croatia, a collection of vegan desserts and healthy recipes for children. Aine currently spends her time between Los Angeles, Ireland and Hawaii.

This recipe can also be prepared with the following variations:
White or wholegrain flour can be used for the dough instead of spelt flour. Other oils can be used instead of coconut oil, even vegetable-based butters. This recipe can also be varied using different fruits depending on the season, such as blackberries, apples, etc.

INGREDIENTS

CRUST
- 2 cups white spelt flour
- 1 cup ground almonds
- 1 tablespoon baking powder
- ¼ tablespoon sea salt
- ½ cup coconut oil
- 1 tablespoon vanilla extract
- 1 tablespoon maple syrup
- ¼ cup cold apple juice

FILLING
- 4 or 5 peaches
- 1 small basket of figs
- 2 tablespoons peach or apricot jam
- ¼ cup apple juice
- 1 tablespoon kuzu or arrowroot

PREPARATION

To make the crust, mix the dry ingredients in a bowl. Add the coconut oil and mix until the mixture acquires the consistency of breadcrumbs. It's best for the coconut oil not to be too liquid nor too solid. Slowly add the vanilla extract and the maple syrup to the cold apple juice and continue mixing until the dough is homogeneous. Cut into two parts and roll them into balls. Press the balls of dough to form a circle and set aside covered in plastic wrap or baking paper for half an hour. Don't put them in the refrigerator, because they will harden and be difficult to roll with the rolling pin.

Heat the oven to 190° C/375° F.

Cut the peaches and figs into slices. Roll out each piece of dough with a rolling pin on the baking paper previously used to cover them making a large circle (they don't have to be perfect, but as close as possible, remember, this is a country pie). Place each circle on a baking tray – you can keep it on the baking paper to transfer it more easily.

Garnish the top of the crust with the sliced figs and peaches, leaving at least 2.5 cm around the edges.

Using the baking paper, turn the edges of the dough upward, around the fruit, folding them.

In a small saucepan, mix the jam and kuzu or arrowroot that has been dissolved in apple juice making sure there are no lumps. Bring to a boil, while stirring, and cook over low heat for 1 minute.

Pour the mixture over the fruit.

Bake for 30 minutes. Then remove from the oven and transfer it to a large serving tray.

The pie is delicious served either hot or cold. Aine McAteer likes to serve it with non-dairy ice cream, or her vanilla and cashew custard.

Olive and dried tomato rolls

These savory rolls go perfectly with a bowl of hot broth or a cream of vegetable soup. Using hemp seeds heightens their nutritional value by adding quality protein with essential fatty acids and fiber. Most food stores stock these seeds, but if you can't find them, use lightly toasted sesame seeds instead, or almonds.

INGREDIENTS

- 1 cup rice flour
- ⅓ cup hulled hemp seeds
- 2 full tablespoons baking powder
- 1 large pinch sea salt
- 1 tablespoon dried oregano
- 50 g diced black olives
- 50 g diced dried tomatoes
- 2 tablespoons freshly chopped parsley
- ¼ cup olive oil
- 1 cup unsweetened soymilk
- Sliced almonds for garnish

PREPARATION

Pre-heat the oven to 180° C/350° F.

Cover a baking tray with baking paper and smear it with oil.

Mix the flour, hemp seeds, yeast, salt and oregano in a bowl. In another bowl, mix the black olives, dried tomatoes, parsley, olive oil and soymilk. Then mix the ingredients from both bowls all together.

Using an ice cream scoop or large spoon, place portions of the mix on the previously prepared baking paper; place, pressing lightly, a teaspoon of sliced almonds on top of each of the portions.

Bake for about 20 minutes. The rolls can be served either hot or cold with a bowl of hot soup. Garnish with roasted almond slices.

At the age of only 20 and while still a student, **Angela Agrati-Prange** opened her first restaurant with some of her young friends. This is where she discovered, developed and cultivated her passion for food as a path to health and a delight for the eyes and palette. Her interest led her to travel to the United States where she earned a degree as a macrobiotic chef in California and specialized in healing cuisine with her great teachers, Herman and Cornelia Aihara.

After gaining two years of experience in the United States, she returned to Europe, where, over the course of the next 25 years, she shared and enriched her knowledge and talent in macrobiotic vegetarian restaurants, at the macrobiotic center in Berlin, at alternative medicine centers and as a private chef for international celebrities.

Agrati-Prange has trained many young chefs, whom she has inspired thanks to her creativity and technique. After almost three years working with the SHA Wellness Clinic as head macrobiotic chef, she decided to return to her native Italy to dedicate herself to teaching healthy cuisine through courses and talks and advising restaurants and cafés. Her extensive knowledge of the subject, her enthusiasm and professionalism have always created fervor and passion for good food among those who participate in her classes.

Kamut and spelt raviolis with boletus sauce and roasted almonds

INGREDIENTS

FOR THE RAVIOLIS:

- 250 g kamut flour
- 250 g white spelt flour
- 1 pinch unrefined sea salt
- 80-100 ml warm water
- 1 tablespoon extra virgin olive oil

FOR THE RAVIOLI FILLING:

- 500 g winter squash
- 1 shallot
- ½ teaspoon unrefined sea salt
- 1 teaspoon extra virgin olive oil
- 1 pinch ground black pepper
- ¼ teaspoon grated nutmeg
- ¼ teaspoon ground cardamom
- 3 teaspoons almond flour
- 1 teaspoon soy sauce
- 1 teaspoon umeboshi vinegar (optional)
- Diced fresh chives
- Crushed roasted almonds

FOR THE SAUCE:

- 200 g fresh boletus mushrooms or other wild mushroom
- 2 shallots or 1 small yellow onion
- 2 sage leaves
- 2 tablespoons extra virgin olive oil
- ½ teaspoon unrefined sea salt
- 1 tablespoon soy sauce
- ¼ cup white wine
- 1 tablespoon soy cream (optional)
- Ground black pepper, to taste

PREPARATION

FOR THE RAVIOLI DOUGH

Mix the two types of flour in a bowl along with the salt. Mix the oil with half of the warm water and slowly pour it over the dry ingredients, gently mixing it by hand.

Add the rest of the water little by little (it may not be necessary to add all of the water) and make a ball of dough that has a solid consistency.

Knead the dough on a flat surface for 5 to 10 minutes or until the dough is soft and elastic.

Wrap it up in plastic wrap and let it sit for at least half an hour.

FOR THE RAVIOLI FILLING

Pre-heat oven to 180° C/350° F.

Finely chop the shallot and set aside. Wash and cut the squash into thick slices and place them in a large bowl, add salt and let sit for 10 minutes. Cover with oil and place on baking tray, adding a few spoonfuls of water. Cover with aluminum foil. Bake in the oven for 20 minutes; afterwards remove the aluminum foil and continue baking until the squash is tender. Meanwhile, heat the oil in a frying pan and sauté the shallot with a pinch of salt for 30 seconds. Add 1 or 2 tablespoons of hot water and let cook over medium heat for 1 minute or until all of the liquid is absorbed.

Place the squash, without skin, in a bowl and mash it with a fork. Add the shallot, nutmeg, cardamom and black pepper and mix well. Season with umeboshi vinegar and soy sauce. Mix in the almond flour to give it a firmer consistency. Taste and adjust the flavor if necessary.

FOR THE SAUCE

Cut the shallots into very thin half moons. Sauté them in a large frying pan with the olive oil for 2 minutes.

Clean the mushrooms and cut them into thin slices. Add the shallots and the sage leaves and sauté over high heat for 1 minute. Add the white wine and the salt. Allow the alcohol to evaporate and cook for 3-4 minutes over low heat. Season with soy sauce and pepper. Add the soy cream and a bit of hot water if necessary.

TO FILL THE RAVIOLIS

Divide the ravioli dough into two parts. Using a rolling pin, roll the dough out on a flat surface that has been lightly dusted with flour until the dough is very thin. Use a pasta cutter to make circles that are 5 cm in diameter.

Place a bit of the filling in the center of each circle. Moisten the edges of the dough with a brush, fold them over and seal them by gently pressing them together with your fingers; repeat the operation with a fork to make an attractive edge. Continue until all of the dough and filling are used. Cook the raviolis in abundant boiling water with salt for 3 minutes.

While still hot, sauté the raviolis in a frying pan with the mushroom sauce. Sprinkle them with diced fresh chives and roasted crushed almonds. Serve hot.

and mix with the previously boiled soymilk. Sweeten with syrup, to taste, and pour it on to a large tray. Keep it in the refrigerator until it chills and solidifies and then beat with a blender until a soft cream is obtained.

SERVING THE DISH
Prepare a cup of strong coffee and sweeten it with syrup. Add sake or mirin. Cut the cake into ½ cm slices and use half of them to cover the bottom of a glass or ceramic tray. Using a brush, soak the cake with half of the coffee and sake mix. Similarly, pour on half of the cream. Cover with the remaining cake, soak with the rest of the coffee and sake and do the same with the rest of the cream. Put in the refrigerator for at least 1 hour. Generously dust with cocoa powder before serving.

Tiramisu

INGREDIENTS

FOR THE CAKE
- 230 ml soymilk
- ½ tablespoon apple vinegar
- 1 ¼ cups white spelt flour
- 2 tablespoons arrowroot
- 1 teaspoon natural yeast
- ½ teaspoon baking soda
- 1 pinch unrefined sea salt
- 80 ml refined sunflower oil
- 180 ml rice syrup
- ½ teaspoon vanilla powder

FOR THE CREAM
- 1 l soy or oat milk
- 150 ml soy cream
- Zest of two lemons
- 2 heaping teaspoons of powdered agar-agar or 4 tablespoons of agar-agar flakes
- 125 ml rice or maple syrup
- 1 pinch unrefined sea salt
- 2 tablespoons arrowroot
- ¼ teaspoon turmeric

TO SERVE
- 1 cup strong coffee (made with coffee beans, not instant coffee)
- 2 tablespoons rice syrup
- 1 tablespoon mirin or sake
- ½ cup sugar-free cocoa powder

PREPARATION

FOR THE CAKE
Pre-heat the oven to 160° C/325° F.
Mix the milk with the apple vinegar in a bowl and set aside for a few minutes.
Sift the flour with the salt, arrowroot, yeast and baking soda into a large bowl.
In another bowl, beat the oil with the syrup for 1 minute. Add the soymilk and mix.
Very slowly, using a spatula, mix the dry with the liquid ingredients until there are no lumps. Pour the mix into a square mold and bake it for 35-40 minutes.

FOR THE CREAM
Mix the milk and the soy cream with the agar-agar, salt, lemon zest and turmeric in a pot. Bring to a boil and let boil over low heat for 8 to 10 minutes, regularly stirring so that it doesn't stick. Dissolve the arrowroot in a small bowl with two tablespoons of cold water

Melanie Brown Waxman teaches wellness and healthy cuisine internationally, is an expert in macrobiotics, healthy nutrition and feng shui, and has 35 years of experience as a coach in the healing arts. Brown Waxman started studying the healing arts in the 1980s, when she specialized in nutritional education and health, macrobiotic cuisine, the energy of foods and other therapies. Her focus on health and healing is shaped by common sense, is easy to apply and is also very realistic. In 2009, she was presented with the Aveline Kushi Award for her long time dedication to macrobiotics and world peace.

She has written several books on health and wellness, such as, *Upbeat Macrobiotic Cooking for Family and Friends*, *Mr. Hoppity's Color Me Cookbook for Kids*, *Bless the Baby*, *Yummy Yummy in My Tummy*, *Eat Me Now!* and *The Little Carrot*.

She is currently part of the SHA Wellness Clinic team.

Mix of marinated vegetables

This recipe is a simple, delicious way to enjoy a variety of colorful vegetables that are full of antioxidants and phytochemicals. It's ideal for the immune system and it provides a light and refreshing energy boost. Try adding your favorite and/or seasonal vegetables to give it touches of different flavors.

INGREDIENTS

- 1 cup cauliflower
- 1 cup broccoli
- ½ cup snow peas or green beans
- 2 carrots thinly cut at an angle
- ½ red pepper, cut in large pieces
- 6 mushrooms, in slices
- 1 cup marinated artichoke hearts, cut in quarters
- ½ cup black olives, in slices
- 4 fresh basil leaves, chopped for garnish

FOR THE DRESSING

- 1 clove garlic, diced
- 3 tablespoons balsamic vinegar
- 2 tablespoons freshly squeezed lemon juice
- 1 tablespoon Dijon mustard
- 1 tablespoon virgin olive oil
- 1 pinch dried oregano
- 1 pinch dried rosemary
- 1 tablespoon brown rice syrup
- ½ teaspoon salt
- ½ teaspoon freshly ground black pepper

PREPARATION

Boil a pot of water.

Add the carrots and blanch for 1 minute. Remove and place on a serving tray.

Repeat with the cauliflower, broccoli, snow peas, pepper and then the mushrooms.

Blanch until the vegetables are slightly tender but still crisp. Blanch each of the vegetables separately.

Remove each of the vegetables and place them on a tray.

Put the ingredients for the sauce in a small bowl and stir until well mixed.

Add the olives and artichokes to the salad.

Then add the dressing and toss gently. Let it sit for 15 minutes, tossing it a few more times.

Serve with fresh basil sprinkles.

Patricia Restrepo is the head of Spain's Instituto Macrobiótico, executive director of Movimiento Alimento S.L., co-founder of the Kimpira restaurant in Valencia, macrobiotic consultant and author.

She has spent the last 25 years studying and promoting the power of meditation, yoga and intelligent nutrition.

She is backed by 35 years of experience in nutrition awareness and 20 years' training chefs, macrobiotic consultants and nutritional therapists.

As a writer, Restrepo periodically contributes to different publications including *Integral*, *Vegetariana* and *Guía Verde Valencia*. She is a regular speaker at conferences and forums on nutrition and natural health in Spain and the Americas. She regularly participates in the program *Salud Natural TV*.

Notable in her long career is having introduced yoga and macrobiotics to the Universidad Politécnica de Valencia and the Universidad de Valencia. She has taught courses on macrobiotic cuisine in the Gastronomy Department of Medellin's Colegiatura Colombiana.

She is currently one of the professors overseeing the master's program in Personal Development and Leadership at the Universidad de Valencia's Fundación Universidad y Empresa (ADEIT).

A well-known consultant, Restrepo's wisdom and closeness touches everyone, inspiring patients to follow the guidelines to achieve extraordinary results.

She played a major part in the revolution of organic and intelligent nutrition in Valencia in the 1990s.

Mother and grandmother, she acknowledges that "her primary master is her daily meditation cushion, and her primary laboratory, the kitchen."

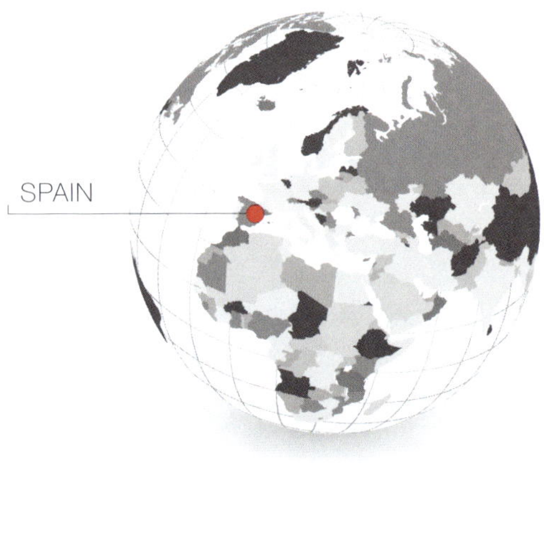

Baked stuffed pumpkin

Stuffed pumpkin is a festive dish that is also very nutritious. It is especially nutritious in winter or for people with blood sugar disorders.

INGREDIENTS

- 1 medium pumpkin
- 1 cup cuscus
- 30 g pilonga chestnuts
- 1 leek, with the green section
- 30 g smoked tofu
- 30 g dried apricots, rehydrated
- 1 red onion
- 1 tablespoon olive oil
- 1 pinch salt
- 3 tablespoons water
- 1 black truffle from Teruel

PREPARATION

Cut the pumpkin in half, clean out the seeds and partially remove the pulp, setting aside the extracted pulp.
Cook the chestnuts in a little water until they are soft (and set aside).
Cut the leeks into rings, including the green section.
Cut the red onion into small cubes and chop the citronella finely.
Sauté the onion, the leeks and the citronella in a frying pan with the oil and a pinch of salt for 5 minutes over high heat. Add the pumpkin, chestnuts and tofu, continue sautéing and finally add the cuscus and the apricot in strips. Stir and add two tablespoons of water.
Stuff the two pumpkin halves, wrap the halves en papillote with rice paper or similar and put in the oven (which has been pre-heated to 250° C/480° F) for 10 minutes. Lower the heat and cook at 200° C/400° F for 40 minutes or until the pumpkin is very soft and the cuscus has been cooked in its own juice.
Serve with grated black truffle.

Gluten-free orange and corn cake

INGREDIENTS

FOR THE BOTTOM LAYER
- 10 gluten-free corn cookies
- 4 tablespoons refined sunflower oil

FOR THE FILLING
- 125 ml yogurt
- 200 ml natural soymilk
- 65 ml refined sunflower oil
- 200 ml rice syrup
- 150 g cornmeal
- 1 teaspoon baking soda
- Orange zest
- 1 pinch salt

FOR THE TOP LAYER
- 250 ml orange juice
- ½ tablespoon agar-agar in flakes
- 1 tablespoon rice syrup

PREPARATION

FOR THE BOTTOM LAYER
Crush the cookies using a rolling pin, add the oil and press into a mold. Bake for 10 minutes at 200° C/400° F. Remove, let cool and set aside.

FOR THE FILLING
Combine all of the liquids (yogurt, soymilk, sunflower oil and syrup) and the salt with a whisk. Mix the cornmeal with the baking soda and the orange zest and slowly add the liquids to this mixture, stir until a cake-like consistency is achieved. Line the mold with baking paper and place the filling inside, place on lowest level of the oven and bake at 140° C/285° F in a convection oven for 30 minutes, directing the air on top of the cake for the last 5 minutes so that the top turns golden brown.

FOR THE TOP LAYER
Dissolve the agar-agar in a bit of water, heat for 5 minutes over high heat, lower the heat for 15 minutes until the agar-agar flakes dissolve, add the orange juice and syrup and set aside.

Put the cake on top of the cookie base in a deep dish, pour the orange cream over the cake and let chill in the refrigerator.

London resident **Simon Brown** is the author of Modern Day Macrobiotics and Macrobiotics For Life. He is a macrobiotic practitioner, consultant and teacher. He offers online and in-person macrobiotic consultations in addition to teaching macrobiotic courses. Brown studied macrobiotics in 1980 in London and later went to the United States to study with Michio Kushi, Aveline Kushi, Shizuko Yamamoto and Denny Waxman. While there, he helped run the Macrobiotic Association of Philadelphia.

After returning to London, Brown became the director of London's Community Health Foundation from 1986 to 1993, a leading macrobiotic center and school in the United Kingdom.

Brown co-authored the book Against All Odds with Dr. Hugh Faulkner, in which he charts his recovery from pancreatic cancer using a macrobiotic diet. He has regularly organized courses by Michio and Aveline Kushi and Shizuko Yamamoto. Brown now organizes annual courses to obtain macrobiotic certification. He is also a member of the Macrobiotic Association, of which he has served as chair. He is furthermore a well-known professional consultant and feng shui teacher. While he was at London's Community Health Foundation, Brown also led the first long courses in feng shui held in the United Kingdom, with William Spear and Takashi Yoshikawa. In 1993, Brown left to fully dedicate himself to his feng shui work in London and around the United Kingdom, Europe and the United States. His feng shui clients include The Body Shop, British Airways, T2G Airport Paris, Torino Airport in Italy and Heron International, as well as companies and corporations, studios, stores, apartments and private properties. Brown is a member of the Feng Shui Society, of which he has also served as president.

Roast vegetables and roots

Roasting is the traditional English way to prepare vegetables. This recipe is warm, nutritious and healthy and, furthermore, very easy to prepare. I especially like its colors, sweet flavor and rich texture. The advantage of roasting vegetables is that they don't lose any of their nutrients in water or oil. Furthermore, the heat of the oven helps make the food's calories more available, giving us more energy on a cold day or when we need an extra energy boost when exercising. Cutting the vegetables into smaller sizes reduces the roasting time. I suggest adding rosemary, although you can add any dried herb to give another dimension to the flavor of this dish; basil, for example, gives it a fresh touch. Any fresh herb can be added later when serving the dish.

INGREDIENTS

- 2 kg mix of beets, carrots, zucchini, pumpkin and parsnips, cut into thick pieces.
- 2 tablespoons dried rosemary
- 2 tablespoons olive oil

PREPARATION

Preheat the oven to 180° C/350° F.
Place the vegetables on a baking tray and mix with the olive oil. Sprinkle the rosemary over the vegetables.
Bake for 20-30 minutes or until soft.

Apple and cookie crumble

Macrobiotics offers a marvelous variety of natural, healthy and delicious desserts that don't require sugar. This is an example of an apple crumble that is very easy and quick to make and which children love. The ingredients are very nutritious and form part of a healthy diet. Experiment with different types of apples or fruits to get other textures and flavors. The crumble can be served with cinnamon, nutmeg, berries or mint leaves.

INGREDIENTS

- 1 kg organic apples and pears (1/2 kg each), cored and cut into pieces
- 60 ml sugar-free jam (choose your favorite flavor)
- 2 200 g packs Bio Malt sugar-free cookies (made by Molenaarjte), or similar
- 50 g sliced almonds

PREPARATION

Preheat the oven to 180° C/350° F.
Place the cut pieces of apple and pear in an oven-safe recipient to cook. Mix them with the jam. Place the cookies on a large piece of cotton cloth and fold the cloth in half. Crush the cookies with a rolling pin until they are reduced to small crumbs. Sprinkle the cookie crumbs over the apples and pears and then do the same with the sliced almonds.
Bake for 20-25 minutes.

Simone Parris has cooked and worked in the health and wellness industry for more than 20 years. The goal of her cooking is to create delicious meals that increase one's health, longevity and awareness, by nourishing the body, mind and spirit.

Parris sees cooking as an art and an expression of love, using the freshest organic ingredients, putting an emphasis on grains, legumes, sea and land vegetables, fruits, nuts and seeds to create a healthy and balanced cuisine with a great variety of flavors and textures to delight the senses.

These dishes are designed for people with very busy lives, to help them stay in shape and full of energy.

Her experience includes catering for large parties and special events, as well as being a chef for clients who want to experience a healthier diet; notable among her clients are Tom Cruise, Nicole Kidman and Steven Segal.

Parris also teaches people to cook and helps them change to a healthier lifestyle through her group or individual classes and cooking workshops.

Sweet Indian carrot pudding

In India, this dessert is prepared in winter when carrots are fresh and juicy. It's an Indian version of carrot cake. This recipe is ideal for the winter: spicy, warm and not too sweet. In India, red carrots are often used, but regular carrots can also be used. I serve it with some nuts to give it more flavor and make the dessert more nutritious.

INGREDIENTS

- 5 tablespoons sunflower oil
- 1 kg grated carrots
- 250 ml sugar-free soy or coconut milk
- 170 ml or 90 g rice syrup
- ¼ cup cardamom powder
- 2 tablespoons raw cashews
- 2 tablespoons raisins
- 1 tablespoon natural rose water (optional)

PREPARATION

Heat the oil in a frying pan with a thick base. Sauté the grated carrots over medium heat (for about 20 minutes) until the water evaporates and the carrots become sweet and dry. Make sure the carrots don't burn, adjusting the heat as necessary. Add the soymilk or coconut milk and continue cooking until all of the liquid, including the milk, is absorbed.

Once the liquid is absorbed, add the cardamom and the rice syrup and continue cooking over low heat for 5 more minutes.

Heat a bit of oil in a small frying pan and sauté the cashews until they are golden brown, remove and sauté the raisins in a bit more oil for a few minutes or until they are golden brown.

Mix the cashews and raisins (and the rose water if used) into the carrot mix and turn off the heat. Use an ice cream scoop to serve and serve at room temperature.

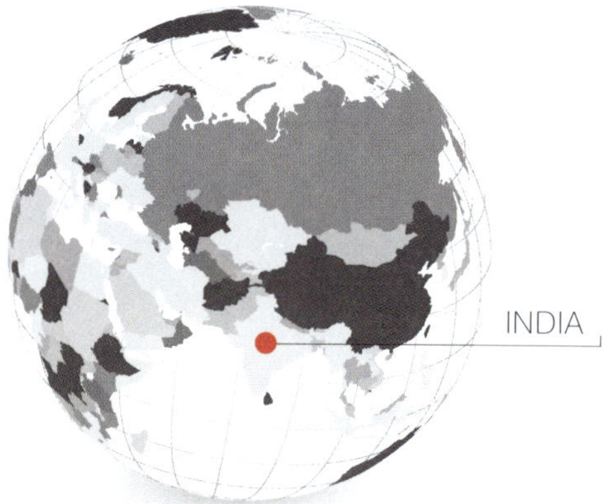

Spicy Indian style seitan with green vegetables

This is a delicious, succulent and substantial dish full of flavor. Green leafy vegetables are full of chlorophyll and fiber and the seitan has a lot of protein and is sufficiently satiating for those looking to replacc animal protein with vegetable protein-based dishes.

INGREDIENTS

- 1 tablespoon extra virgin olive oil
- 2 cups onions cut into thin half moons
- 1 tablespoon crushed or diced garlic
- 1 tablespoon peeled and diced ginger
- 1 tablespoon coriander seeds, roasted and ground (or else purchase this spice ready-to-use)
- ¼ tablespoon red chili powder
- 1 pinch garam masala
- 1 tablespoon natural shoyu soy sauce
- 2 tablespoons mirin or Chinese cooking wine
- Sea salt, to taste
- Fresh black pepper, to taste
- Seitan cut into bite-sized cubes
- Spinach, Swiss chard, collard greens or kale, carefully washed and blanched in lightly salted boiling water for 2 minutes (if using collard greens or kale, cut into thin strips before blanching), drain and cut into thin strips
- Soy cream for garnish
- Fresh coriander or scallions, washed, dried and sliced thinly as garnish

PREPARATION

Heat the oil in a covered frying pan and sauté the onions for about 5 minutes with a pinch of sea salt. Mix in the seitan, garlic, ginger, chili powder, salt and ground coriander seeds and sauté for another 2 minutes. Add the shoyu soy sauce, mirin or Chinese cooking wine and a cup of water (about 110 ml), cover and lower the heat; cook over low heat for 15 minutes.

Remove the cover and add the blanched vegetables, another pinch of sea salt, black pepper and continue cooking the mix until the excess liquid disappears.

Sprinkle on the garam masala and soy cream and garnish the dish. Serve hot and enjoy!

SUGGESTIONS

You can buy wholegrain wheat seitan and spelt seitan can also be found and is worth trying. It tends to be more tender and flavorful. Spelt has a bit less protein, but it is also easier to digest.

Kidney bean salad

This recipe can be made with any type of bean, red, white, etc. For a spicy touch, add freshly grated ginger at the end of the cooking process. This dish is a good source of protein and minerals.

INGREDIENTS

- 2 cups pre-soaked kidney beans
- 2 leeks
- 2 carrots
- 1 small zucchini
- 1 sheet pre-soaked kombu seaweed
- 1 pinch salt
- 1 dash sesame oil or olive oil
- Chopped coriander
- Chopped chives or parsley

PREPARATION

Cook the beans with the kombu in water for 30 minutes or until tender. In a separate saucepan, heat a little sesame oil and sauté the white section of the leeks along with the carrots for 10 minutes.

Add the beans, the zucchini cut into small cubes, and some salt. Add a bit of the water used to cook the beans. Cook for another 10 minutes and then add the chopped chives or parsley.

Geninha Horta Varatojo is one of the most well-known cooking teachers in Portugal and the author of four books: *Cozinha Natural-Deliciosas Receitas Macrobióticas*, *Macro Apetite*, *Memória dos Sabores* and *Tudo o que comemos conta*. She also regularly teaches courses in Spain and has written numerous articles for both Portuguese and Spanish magazines over the past 20 years.

Horta Varatojo is the mother of four children (brought up according to macrobiotic principles) and is particularly interested in such subjects as education and child nutrition. Along with her husband Francisco, she founded the Instituto Kushi in Portugal and is currently the head of cooking programs at Instituto Macrobiótico de Portugal.

Garbanzo bean stew

INGREDIENTS

- 1 soup bowl of cooked garbanzo beans
- 2 onions
- 1 carrot
- 1 slice pumpkin
- 2 cloves garlic
- 3 tablespoons olive oil
- 1 tablespoon umeboshi vinegar
- 1 pinch salt
- Fresh coriander, chives and thyme

PREPARATION

Sauté the onions, garlic and chopped thyme in a saucepan with the olive oil. Add the carrot and the pumpkin which has been cut into small cubes. Add a bit of the water used to cook the garbanzo beans, cover the saucepan and let boil over low heat for 10 to 15 minutes.

Add the garbanzo beans, season with salt and umeboshi vinegar and boil over low heat for another 10 minutes. If any liquid is left, thicken it with arrowroot diluted in cold water.

Serve with chopped coriander or chives.

Strawberry mousse

INGREDIENTS

- 1 kg strawberries
- ½ l water (or apple juice)
- 1 tablespoon agar-agar
- rice syrup
- 1 teaspoon vanilla
- 1 teaspoon grated lemon zest
- Mint leaves

PREPARATION

Wash the strawberries well and cut them up. Boil the agar-agar in water for 5 to 10 minutes or until completely dissolved.

Add the rice syrup, vanilla and lemon zest and pour the mix over the strawberries. Let cool and mix with a blender until thick, smooth and creamy. Serve in dessert bowls and garnish with a whole strawberry and a mint leaf.

You can also cut the strawberries and put them in small gelatin cubes instead of blending them. It's quite refreshing and aromatic.

Gala Restrepo (Gala Bernal) was born into a macrobiotic family, the daughter of Patricia Restrepo, whose surname she has adopted. Starting in her early childhood, Gala Restrepo interiorized an interest in healthy cooking and made it her own.

As an adult, Restrepo studied at the Instituto Macrobiótico de España, as well as at the Kushi Institute. She now hosts the television program *La cocina de Gala, la cocina sana* in Colombia. She lives between Colombia and Miami providing consultations on macrobiotic nutrition. Restrepo, in addition, teaches at the Instituto Macrobiótico de España several times a year.

Peruvian yam *causa* and vegan tuna

Causa is a unique dish that is part of Peruvian cuisine and which is normally prepared with *papa criolla* (Andean potatoes). This recipe, however, uses yams for their nutritional properties, given that they are rich in collagen and ideal for restoring the skin's tone and reducing the symptoms of menopause.

This dish is served cold as a starter or as a light meal.

INGREDIENTS

- 1 yam
- The pulp left over from the juice of 5 carrots
- 2 sheets of nori seaweed
- 2 onions cut into small cubes
- Juice of 2 lemons
- 200 ml soymilk
- 350 ml sunflower oil
- 2 avocadoes
- ½ teaspoon umeboshi
- Chopped fresh coriander
- Coriander flower
- 1 dash olive oil
- Chutney
- Salt

FOR THE *CAUSA*

Cook the yam in a pressure cooker for 30 minutes until it's soft and then purée it with a dash of olive oil and salt to taste.

FOR THE SEA MAYONNAISE

Put the soymilk, sunflower oil, the juice of half a lemon and the nori seaweed in a blender, add salt to taste and blend until the mixture has the texture of mayonnaise.

FOR THE VEGAN TUNA

Juice 5 carrots in a juicer and set aside the leftover pulp. Blend the onion with a pinch of salt and half a lemon. Add the carrot pulp and the mayonnaise. Mix all of the ingredients well.

FOR THE GUACAMOLE

Blend the avocado, add the blended onion, lemon, coriander, salt to taste and a teaspoon of umeboshi paste.

SERVING THE DISH

Start with a layer of yam followed by a layer of vegan tuna and then add a layer of guacamole on top. Serve with mayonnaise and chutney. Garnish with coriander flowers.

Mieke Vervecken, mother of six children between 32 and 22 years of age, began her relationship with macrobiotics and yoga at the age of 18, after a serious illness.

Vervecken has 44 years of experience cooking. She has studied in Antwerp, London, Switzerland, the United States and Japan. She started The Natural Cookery School in 1990 to offer full macrobiotic culinary training and to train cooks. She has worked on numerous projects, written articles for the press and appeared on television.

From 1998 to 2010, she was the head chef of ROSAS-P.A.R.T.S., Anne Teresa De Keersmaeker's internationally famous dance company and school, in Brussels. She trained the chefs at the Lerab Ling Buddhist Center in France and is today very active as a consultant and private chef in the Middle East.

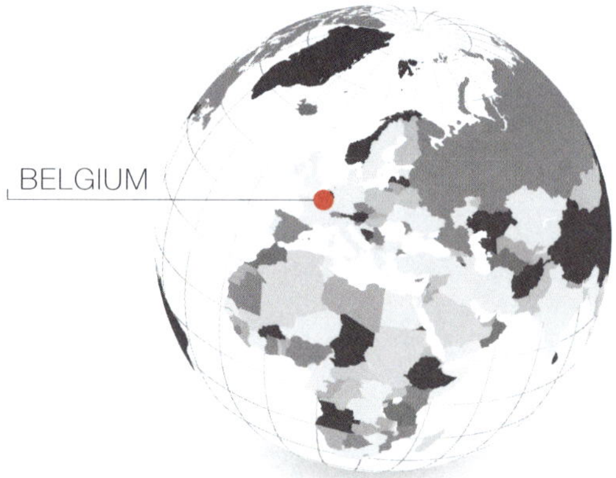

Vervecken is appreciated for her enthusiasm, creativity and knowledge of Japanese cuisine.

"My passions: cooking and taking care of my family and friends. I enjoy nature; I am inspired by taking walks in the woods near my house the silence of the desert. I like languages, their poetry and people. I speak English, French and German fluently and I'm learning Arabic. Nature and people inspire my creativity and my healthy cuisine."

Vegetable stir fry

Wok cooking with a has many health benefits; it preserves all of the vitamins and minerals and increases our "fiery" energy. It also allows us to quickly prepare a very nutritious dish. Vegetables remain crunchy and we can either use water or dashi (stock) and oil to cook them. We can also add ingredients that give extra flavor, some of which have medicinal effects, such as ginger, which helps circulation and reduces swelling; garlic, which is good for the circulatory system; lemon or orange zest, which helps break down animal protein; or fresh lotus root, which helps loosen mucus and can aid in clearing the lungs.

For more flavor, you can add miso or soy, and for an even more intense flavor, try adding lemon juice or rice vinegar or mirin. In winter, I love adding ginger and mustard. Including some hijiki seaweed in this dish will not only give it more flavor but it will also add extra minerals.

Adding water or dashi when cooking with a wok prevents the oil from becoming too hot and burning.

Use seasonal vegetables or those that suit your taste.

For protein, you can add fried tofu (cut into thin slices and fried), although this can be substituted for tempeh or seitan. In winter, try smoked tofu or tempeh, which will heat the body and add a delicious touch. Pieces of fish or kidney beans can be added as well.

INGREDIENTS

- Vegetables: ½ carrot, ½ onion, 6 thin slices of lotus root, ¼ sweet pepper, 1 head napa cabbage, 6 broccoli florets, 2 endives, 2 leaves watercress, a sprig of fresh coriander... You decide!
- 2 tablespoons dashi stock
- 1 tablespoon olive or sesame oil
- 1 teaspoon fresh grated ginger
- 1 clove garlic
- 1 pinch salt
- 1 tablespoon sliced almonds or walnuts
- 1 teaspoon white miso
- 2 teaspoons lemon juice
- 1 teaspoon mirin
- Soy sauce, to taste
- 50 g somen noodles
- 2 tablespoons hijiki seaweed
- Fresh coriander, to taste
- 40 g tofu
- 2 tablespoons kombu
- Bean sprouts, to taste

PREPARATION

Make a broth by boiling a cup of water with the kombu.

Cut the vegetables thinly; the harder the vegetable, the thinner it should be sliced; leafy vegetables can be cut into 4 or 5 cm pieces.

Put 2 tablespoons of dashi into the wok, along with a tablespoon of olive oil or sesame oil.

Add the grated ginger and a clove of finely diced garlic.

Heat the wok and when it's hot, add the hardest vegetables, such as the carrots and the onions. Add a bit of salt and stir.

One minute later, add the fresh lotus root, broccoli, napa cabbage, endives, watercress, sweet peppers and almonds and continue to stir.

Add the tofu and continue stirring.

One minute later, add the white miso, lemon juice and mirin.

Afterwards add a bit of hijiki and somen noodles.

If all of the water has evaporated, add a bit more of the prepared broth.

Add the coriander, the sprouts and a few drops of soy sauce, stir two or three times more and the dish is complete.

Apple beignets

A special dish for celebrations. When we were children, we liked to eat apples after harvesting them from trees during the month of September. I like to use buckwheat flour, which is a staple food in De Kempen, a region in northern Belgium. Frying is a cooking method that gives us strength and helps satiate us. To balance our the oil, we will use acidic apples.

INGREDIENTS

- 4 apples, cored and cut into 2 cm slices. Tart or billersweet apples are the best
- Frying oil

FOR THE BATTER

- ½ cup buckwheat flour
- 1 pinch salt
- ¼ cup cornstarch
- ¼ cup white spelt flour
- 1 bottle cold beer
- 2 tablespoons vegetable oil
- Optional: buckwheat flakes to sprinkle on top of the batter
- Garnish: 1 tablespoon apple concentrate and a few drops of gin and 1 fresh green wasabi leaf

PREPARATION

Prepare the apples.

Prepare the batter: First mix the dry ingredients, later add the other ingredients and mix well. The batter should easily slide off the spoon.

Heat the oil to 180° C/350° F.

Dip the apples into the batter and (optionally) the buckwheat flakes, and fry them until golden brown. Serve on a plate with the garnish.

Patricio García de Paredes was introduced to macrobiotic food at the age of five by his mother in his native Spain. Patricio is today director of Education at the Kushi Institute of Japan, where he regularly teaches macrobiotics and gives cooking classes. He was the head chef at five of the macrobiotic restaurants to recently open in Tokyo, Japan. Patricio is also the author of various macrobiotic cookbooks.

Patricio keeps a busy international agenda, traveling from his home in Japan where he lives with his wife and their five children.

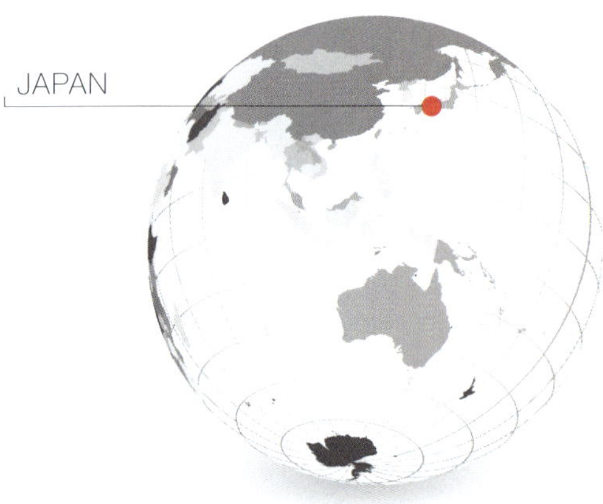

Apple pie with chestnut sauce and blueberry compote

BENEFITS

This apple pie is a good example of the infinite possibilities for preparing nutritious and healthy desserts using natural and healthy ingredients. The sweeteners used are natural and unprocessed and, therefore, help to maintain balanced blood sugar levels. Using quality, unprocessed vegetable oils in the crust helps reduce the use of butter, which contains saturated fats, or margarines, which contain hydrogenated fats.

INGREDIENTS

FOR THE CRUST
- 200 g wholegrain pastry flour
- 2 pinches aluminum-free baking powder
- 1 pinch sea salt
- 65 ml unprocessed sesame oil
- 50 ml apple juice, or as much as needed

FOR THE FILLING
- 700 g apples
- 50 ml pure maple syrup
- 15 ml freshly squeezed lemon juice
- 1 pinch ground cinnamon
- 1 pinch sea salt
- 3 g kuzu or arrowroot in powder

FOR THE CHESTNUT SAUCE
- 50 g cooked chestnuts
- 100 ml water
- 50 ml soymilk
- 30 ml pure maple syrup
- 2 g kuzu or arrowroot powder

- 4 cm vanilla bean
- 1 pinch sea salt

FOR THE BLUEBERRY COMPOTE

- 70 g fresh blueberries
- 60 ml sugar-free blueberry jam
- 100 ml apple juice
- 1 pinch sea salt

PREPARATION

FOR THE FILLING

Peel and core the apples and cut them into small cubes. Bring the maple syrup, lemon juice, cinnamon and salt to a boil in a saucepan. Add the apples and cook over high heat for a few minutes while stirring. Cover the saucepan and lower the heat to a minimum and cook for another 15 minutes or until the apples are soft. Uncover and cook over medium heat until the liquid evaporates. Dissolve the kuzu in a bit of water and add it little by little while stirring the contents of the saucepan. Cook a bit longer while stirring constantly and then let cool and set aside. Divide the apple filling into 10 portions.

FOR THE PIE

Place the flour, baking powder and salt in a bowl and mix well. Add the oil and mix well, kneading by hand. Add the apple juice little by little while mixing until the dough is firm. Flatten the dough with a rolling pin over a sheet of plastic wrap until the dough is 2 mm thick, then cut using a 10 cm diameter circle. Place a portion of the apple filling in the center of each circle, fold the edges of the circle upward and press the edges with your fingertips. Repeat the process until you have made 10 pies. Place the pies on a lined baking tray and bake in a pre-heated oven at 180° C/350° F for 20 minutes or until golden brown.

FOR THE CHESTNUT SAUCE

Chop the chestnuts and place them in a saucepan with water, maple syrup and a pinch of salt. Cut the vanilla bean in half and add it to the saucepan and bring to a boil. Cover, lower the heat and cook for 15 minutes. Remove the vanilla bean and blend the ingredients until the mix is creamy. Put the mix back into the saucepan. Dissolve the kuzu in a bit of water, add it to the sauce and bring to a gentle boil while stirring. Add the soymilk and again bring to a gentle boil while stirring. Afterwards, let chill in a boil on top of some ice water, all the while still stirring the sauce, and then set aside.

FOR THE COMPOTE

Put the blueberry jam, apple juice and salt in a saucepan and bring to a boil while stirring. Lower the heat and let boil for a few minutes. Strain it through a fine sieve, add the blueberries and mix well. Afterwards, let cool in a bowl on top of some ice water while stirring it, and then set aside.

PRESENTATION

Place a spoonful of chestnut sauce on a plate, put the apple pie on top of it and garnish with a few blueberries.

SUGGESTIONS

All of the parts can be prepared beforehand and the apple pie lightly heated in the oven when you want to serve it.

glossary

GLOSSARY OF MACROBIOTIC PRODUCTS USED AT SHA

a

Agar-agar
A white gelatin derived from seaweed, used to prepare kanten and aspic jellies. It comes in bars, flakes and powder.

Arame
Thin, wiry seaweed similar to hijiki. It is generally cooked as a garnish for dishes.

Adzuki (bean)
A small, dark red bean imported from Japan but which is also grown in Spain. Adzuki beans are especially good when cooked with kombu seaweed. They have fortifying properties for the kidneys and gallbladder.

b

Bancha
(tea, also known as hojicha)
Bancha tea consists of the stems and leaves from mature Japanese tea bushes. Bancha tea aids in digestion. It contains no chemical dyes. Bancha makes an excellent after-dinner beverage. It's rich in calcium, vitamin C and antioxidants.

Brown rice
Wholegrain rice. It comes in three main varieties: short, medium and long grain. Brown rice contains the ideal balance of minerals, proteins and carbohydrates.

Buckwheat
Eaten as a staple food in many European countries, this grain is eaten widely in the form of kasha (a type of mash), whole groats and soba noodles.

Burdock
A wild, hardy plant that grows throughout the United States. This long, dark root is highly valuable in macrobiotic cooking for its strengthening qualities, and because it helps purify the blood.

d

Daikon
A long, white radish. Besides making a delicious side dish, daikon is a specific aid in dissolving fat and mucus deposits that have accumulated as a result of past animal food intake. Grated daikon aids in the digestion of oily foods. Dried daikon is effective at dissolving fats stored in the body that are difficult to eliminate.

Dulse
A reddish-purple seaweed that is used in soups, salads and vegetable dishes and is very high in iron.

g

Gomashio
A condiment made from roasted, ground sesame seeds and sea salt. Rich in calcium.

h

Hijiki
A dark brown seaweed that turns black when dried. It has a wiry consistency and may be strong tasting. Hijiki is imported from Japan but also grows off the coast of Maine. Proportionally, it has 10 times more calcium than milk.

Himalayan sea salt
This salt regulates water content throughout the body. It promotes a healthy pH balance in cells, particularly brain cells. It can balance blood sugar levels, help reduce the signs of aging and aid the absorption of food particles through the intestinal tract. It keeps the respiratory tract and circulatory system healthy and strengthens the bones.

i

Ito soba
A very thin, short buckwheat noodle.

k

Kombu
A wide, thick, dark green seaweed that grows in deep ocean water. Used in making soup stocks, condiments, candy and cooked with vegetables and beans.

Kombu (tea)
Derived from powdered kombu and used to prepare a tea that helps calm and balance the nervous system.

Kukicha
Usually called twig bancha tea, this tea consists of the oldest stems and leaves of the Japanese tea bush. High in vitamin C, calcium and anti-oxidants. (See Bancha)

Kuzu
A white starch made from the root of the wild kuzu plant. In the United States, the plant is called "kudzu." It is used in making soups, sauces, desserts and for medicinal purposes. It strengthens the intestines and is alkaline.

l

Lotus root
The root of the water lily, which is brown-skinned with a hollow, chambered, off-white inside. Especially good for respiratory organs.

m

Millet
This small, yellow grain comes in many varieties and can be eaten on a regular basis. It can be used in soups, vegetable dishes or eaten as a cereal. It's the only alkaline wholegrain.

Miso (genmai)
Miso made from fermented brown rice, soybeans and sea salt. It is sometimes referred to as brown rice miso.

Miso (yellow shiro)
Miso fermented for a short period of time, with a very mild flavor. It's made from a mix of koji rice, soybeans, rice and sea salt.

Mu (tea)
A tea made from nine or 16 different herbs. It has certain medicinal values, such as its ability to warm the body and strengthen female reproductive organs. Contains ginseng.

n

Nori
Thin sheets of seaweed that are dark purple when dried. They are roasted over a flame until they turn green. They are used as a garnish, wrapped around rice balls when preparing sushi, or cooked with tamari soy sauce and enjoyed as a condiment. Nori flakes can be used as a seasoning, sprinkled over a meal.

r

Rice syrup
Natural sweetener obtained from cooked, fermented rice that transforms rice starch into sugars. This dense, sweet syrup can be used like honey, molasses or other liquid sweeteners. With a bit of planning, it can also substitute granulated sugar.

S

Sesame oil

This oil obtained from sesame seeds is rich in nutrients and is popular in alternative medicine. It is used in traditional massages and treatments as well as in modern diets. According to traditional medicine in India, sesame oil is believed to calm the systems related to stress and current studies indicate that the notable presence of antioxidants and polyunsaturated fats in sesame oil can help regulate blood pressure.

Shiitake

A dried, medicinal mushroom imported from Japan.

Soba

Noodles made from buckwheat flour or a combination of buckwheat with wholegrain wheat flour.

Soy sauce (tamari)

Tamari is the name given by George Ohsawa to traditional, naturally made soy sauce to distinguish it from the commercial, chemically processed variety. The original term *tamari* refers to a thick, condensed liquid that results from the process of making miso at the moment when the water rises to the surface. This is poured off and called tamari.

Soybean (black)

This is a soybean variety. Nutritionally, black soybeans are very similar to yellow soybeans. They are high in fiber and protein and are relatively low in carbohydrates.

Shimeji

The term *shimeji* refers to a group of edible mushrooms native to East Asia, but also found in northern Europe. The hon-shimeji (*Lyophyllum shimeji*) is difficult to cultivate, and the buna shimeji is now widely cultivated. Shimeji mushrooms are rich in umami tasting compounds and have a pleasant flavor.

Shiso

The term *shiso* is the Japanese name for *Perilla frutescens*, a plant that is currently highly valued for its culinary uses and which was widely used in Oriental cultures for medicinal purposes; it is also used as an ornamental plant. Rich in minerals and vitamins and with anti-inflammatory properties, shiso is also thought to help preserve and sterilize other foods. There are two main varieties, red or purple, and green. Red shiso has a flavor similar to cumin. The most common shiso is green, known as *aojiso*.

t

Tekka

A condiment obtained from sautéing hatcho miso, sesame oil, burdock, lotus root, carrot and ginger root for several hours over low heat.

u

Udon

Japanese noodles made from wholegrain wheat flour or wholegrain wheat flour with unbleached white flour.

Umeboshi

A salty and sour pickled plum, traditionally used to improve digestion. Umeboshi is very alkaline and is used in cases of food poisoning, heartburn and as a natural antibiotic.

V

Vinegar (rice vinegar)

A mild vinegar made from brown rice. It helps balance the liver and gallbladder.

Vinegar (umeboshi vinegar)

Umeboshi vinegar isn't really a vinegar, but rather the liquid produced by the fermentation of umeboshi plums. Used for cooking and as a salad dressing.

W

Wakame

A long, thin, green seaweed used in making soups, salads, vegetable dishes, etc.

GLOSSARY OF UTENSILS, APPLIANCES AND COOKING TECHNIQUES

Kinpira

Kinpira is a Japanese cooking style in which food is "sautéed and simmered." Traditionally used to cook carrots and burdock, this simple technique can be used in many different ways, combining different vegetables, roots and even vegetable proteins such as tofu, seitan or tempeh, or using seaweed. In the kinpira style, vegetables are cut thinly and small, while roots are cut into little sticks. The word kinpira, therefore, means the combination of a cooking style with a specific way of cutting the ingredients.

Mandoline slicer

A kitchen utensil used to easily slice vegetables, etc., into a uniform thickness. There are different types of mandoline slicers that are capable of cutting finely *à la julienne* or that can cut thin sheets of onion, turnip, celery, etc.

Pacojet

A professional kitchen appliance used to process all types of frozen food (generally to make ice creams).

Parmentier

A cooking technique that consists of emulsifying vegetables with fats.

Quenelle

This is the shape generally given to certain sweet and savory culinary blends. To form a quenelle, use two soup spoons and shape a croquette without rounding off the ends.

Silpat

A greaseless, non-stick silicone mat used for baking.

Suribachi

A Japanese ceramic mortar with a rough inner surface that has grooves to aid grinding. The suribachi is ideal for making gomashio.

Surikogi

The pestle used with the Japanese suribachi mortar. It is generally made of cypress or ash.

Verderol 5, Playa del Albir, 03581 Alicante (Spain)
info@shawellnessclinic.com
www.shawellnessclinic.com

Creation and production: Lunwerg, 2018
ISBN: 978-84-08-16001-4
Legal deposit: B 11056-2016
Printed by: Talleres Gráficos Soler

First printing: September 2016
Second printing: November 2018

Lunwerg is an imprint of Editorial Planeta, S.A.
Avenida Diagonal, 662-664 - 08034 BARCELONA
Calle Josefa Valcárcel, 42 - 2ª 28027 Madrid
lunwerg@lunwerg.com
www.lunwerg.com
www.facebook.com/lunwerg
http://twitter.com/Lunwergfoto

Printed in Spain

The paper used in printing this book is 100% chlorine-free and qualifies as ecological paper.